What's wrong with charity?

How modern charity practices are undermining our communities, democracy and public trust

ISBN-13: 978-1500682187

ISBN-10: 1500682187

Waye Forward (publishing)
www.publishing.wayeforward.com
info@wayeforward.com

Waye Forward Ltd is company limited by shareholding (07712660) registered in England and Wales. registered office: 10 Shaftesbury Close, Thornhill, Cardiff CF14 9EJ.

About the author

Tim Watkins is a founder-director of Waye Forward, a Cardiff-based company established to provide support services to innovative charities, social enterprises and small businesses.

Tim Watkins graduated from the University of Wales College Cardiff with a first class honours economics degree in 1990. Between 1990 and 1997 he worked as a policy research officer for the Welsh Consumer Council where he researched and wrote a range of policy reports including *In Deep Water* an investigation into problems in the aftermath of the North Wales ("Towyn") floods of 1990, and *Quality of Life and Quality of Service* an investigation into the promotion of quality of life in residential homes for older people.

Following a severe and enduring episode of depression between 1997 and 2000, Tim Watkins began working for the charity Depression Alliance, running its Wales office, and steering it to becoming an independent charity in its own right in 2005. He continued to run the charity (which re-launched as "Journeys" in 2008) until 2010. During that time, the Welsh Government appointed him to sit on the Health & Wellbeing Council for Wales and the Burrows-Greenwell Review of Mental Health in Wales. He also played a key role in developing the Healthy Minds at Work project, during which he wrote *Taking Control*, an audio self-help book for people affected by depression, and oversaw the development of the award-winning Depression Busting self-management programme for people affected by depression.

In October 2010, along with Julia Kaye and Paul Clarke, Tim Watkins formed Life Surfing CIC as a more honest vehicle to address public wellbeing in people experiencing stress or whose life circumstances put them at risk of developing mental illness and people experiencing mild/moderate common mental illnesses such as anxiety and depression.

Contents

A growing sense of unease

Charity – the voluntary giving of one's time or money to alleviate suffering, to improve the conditions of our fellows for the common good – has been a key element of civil society for centuries. However, at the beginning of the 21st century a series of scandals has created growing unease about contemporary charities. It appears that our charities are poorly regulated by an under-resourced Charity Commission and an indifferent HMRC. They are open to abuse from tax evaders, fraudsters, terrorists and money launderers.

Barely a month goes by without an employee or a trustee being caught syphoning charity funds into their own pockets. And there is growing concern about just how representative charities are – and whose interests they really represent – when they engage in campaigning activities.

Charities, we have been told, should be more "business-like". However, it is my contention that many of the ills within charities have been caused by the drive to emulate the practices of businesses that ultimately put personal gain ahead of all else. In fact, becoming more "business-like" would be a grave threat to the overwhelming majority of charities that neither trade nor employ paid staff. For around 125,000 of the 163,700 registered charities in England and Wales, the aim is not to create employment or to earn profits to distribute to shareholders, but to mobilise voluntary resources to address a social problem that the state has ignored and the market cannot meet without making a loss.

There is certainly room for charities and community groups to become more "professional" in the way they operate. Indeed, the internet, social media and continuous technological improvements bring professional practices much closer to even the smallest community group. However, being professional is something very different to being business-like. Rather, the majority of charities need to learn from the mistakes made by the "business-like" charities in order to develop a new, post-austerity model of charity.

The headlong march to being "business-like" seriously threatens the two elements of charity that make it unique:

o Voluntarism – that the operation of charity is carried out freely and for no material reward for any of those involved.
o Public benefit – that charity always and only serves the public benefit by meeting the needs of the public as a whole, or of a defined community within the general public.

As these recede into the background, we are left struggling to define "charity" as something different either from private businesses or public services. And if (as is increasingly the case) there is no discernable difference, why should charities be treated differently, for example through a generous tax regime and favourable status within public debates?

We have been encouraged to think about the myriad organisations that occupy civil society in terms of three sectors:

o Private sector businesses carry out those activities (the production and sale of goods and services) that can be traded
o The public sector provides those socially necessary public utilities and services that are either too big, costly or loss-making to be universally provided by private business
o The third sector (a mish-mash of informal community groups and associations, co-ops, charities, social enterprises and not for profit companies) picks up all of the other socially necessary activities that cannot be or currently are not provided by the private or public sector.

Regrettably, this distinction becomes ever more meaningless by the day. The modern public sector is little more than a public shop front behind which private business and third sector organisations provide the services for financial gain. The "efficiency" (some would call it profiteering) that successive governments claim this brings is bought at the cost of democratic accountability as service providers hide their activities behind the cloak of "commercial confidentiality" until some scandal erupts (A4E, G4S, Serco, etc). Unfortunately, many charities and social enterprises are also being exposed for "misspending" (often a polite name for fraud) public funds.

Third sector organisations are so varied in their type, size, turnover and operations that it makes no sense trying to distinguish them from any other form of private organisation. The things that used to distinguish the third sector from the rest – voluntarism, public benefit, non-profit, etc – are no longer always present. In terms of providing a socially necessary service, the proprietor of the local corner shop is more "charitable" and provides a greater local benefit than the majority of modern third sector entities.

As we lose track of what we understood by "charity", so we see a growing number of cases of fraud and mismanagement. At the time of writing, the media are reporting on scandal after scandal in the third sector[1].

However, we are still at the "one rotten apple" stage in this unfolding story. Public trust in charities remains high

---

[1] At the time of writing, investigations into the Cup Trust are on-going. The Internet based Charity Giving website has collapsed with small charities owed more than £250,000 in donations made through the site. A recycling scheme raising money for the Variety Club has been exposed as a money-making scheme for a private recycling company, which donated just £5,500 from the £1.9 million raised. In Wales – arguably the fraud capital of the UK – a publicly-funded recycling scheme is under investigation after writing off £2 million in loans made to companies owned by one of its trustees. In the local media around the UK, we also find a steady trickle of minor fraud and mismanagement stories.

and where scandals occur the tendency is to blame corrupt individuals rather than to question what it is about the contemporary charity sector that provides such rich pickings for the fraudulent and sheltered employment for the incompetent.

Just as so-called "light touch" regulation allowed fraud and corruption to infect the banking sector from top to bottom, so a combination of poor legislation, absence of regulation, improper funding systems, and a lack of public awareness have combined to destroy the very things that for centuries made charity such an important part of the fabric of civil society.

I write this book as someone who believes that (when run properly) charity provides the essential cement that can hold the fabric of our society together. In setting out what I believe is wrong with contemporary charities, I seek not to undermine the concept of charity, but rather to return to charity those elements that make it so important.

Having worked in the "third sector" for more than a decade, from direct experience and from knowledge of the research carried out by others, I can assure the reader that fraud and mismanagement within the charity sector is cultural and goes well beyond the "one or two rotten apples" that defenders claim (and anyway, let us not forget that it only takes one or two rotten apples to poison the whole barrel). A growing proportion of modern charities have become both self-serving and highly harmful to the public good. If this is allowed to continue, the growing weight of scandals will undermine the ideal of charity itself. If we allow this to happen, then something that has been at the heart of our social fabric for centuries will die, and with its passing we will all be much worse off.

In this book I set out why we need to examine the system that creates fraud and mismanagement rather than treating each case as if it were solely caused by corrupt or incompetent individuals. I will argue that there are seven interweaving processes within the contemporary charity sector that are conspiring to create a massive – often bureaucratic – "infrastructure of welfare" that undermines the very notion of charity itself:

1. Poor legislation and a lack of regulation
2. The end of voluntarism and the growth of employment within charities
3. Increased fraud and corruption
4. Tax avoidance
5. The creation of "astroturf", "sock puppet" and "moral entrepreneur" charities to hi-jack public discourse
6. The growth of business-emulating charities
7. The problem of charities investing in the corporations and states that cause suffering in the first place.

I will examine each of these in turn to show how modern charity practice is conspiring with an increasingly authoritarian state to undermine the public good.

In the last part of this book, I will set out what I think

needs to be done to set charity back onto a course that serves the long-term public good (even where this is at odds with the whims of the government of the day or the personal interests of those who work within the charity sector).

Historical background

For centuries, charity was primarily about alleviating poverty. In pre-industrial Britain, charity was dispensed at a parish level, where abuse was difficult because people within the parish knew one another and understood each other's circumstances. Industrialisation undermined this system in two ways. First, the migration of labour broke the bonds of trust that existed within villages and parishes. As is the case today, there were just enough people prepared to cheat the system (the "undeserving poor") to undermine it for everyone else.

However, as is the case today, the second and much more serious problem was corruption among those charged with administering charity. It became all too common for those who ran the system to simultaneously plunder it to the point that even conservative Victorian Britain was forced to take action.

An investigation into the state of charities eventually led to the Charitable Trusts Act of 1853 and the establishment of a new Charity Commission to register and regulate charity and, hopefully, to curb the worst excesses.

Most of what we now understand as charity was fashioned by common law rather than statute, most notably in the Pemsel Case of 1891 in which Lord McNaughton classified "charity" into four key areas (or "Heads of Charity"):

- The alleviation of poverty
- The promotion of education
- The promotion of health
- The promotion of religion.

Anything falling outside these four areas could not be charitable.

By the end of the 19th century, the state was flexing its muscles, and shifting into ground traditionally claimed by charity. Two changes in 1870 paved the way for the gradual development of the 20th century welfare state. First, and most well-known, is the Education Act, which cleared the way for the provision of state education. Second, catastrophically for the Poor Law, was a move to allow women to sit on the Boards of Poor Law Guardians. This resulted in abuse – in an echo of modern workfare, it was not uncommon for these women to "recruit" destitute young women to work as their household servants in conditions that amounted to little more than slavery.

Much more serious was the shift in Poor Law philosophy that the idle wives of the industrial rich brought with them onto the Boards of Guardians. For centuries, poor relief had been based around the village or the parish (today we would call it "community"). From 1870, this shifted to a system based on the family. For the first time, widows were marched off to workhouses when their surviving relatives proved unable to support them and the Poor Law refused to pay an allowance. People disabled in work related accidents were no longer provided for. And, in Dickensian fashion, the children of the urban poor were forced to beg or thieve.

Labour campaigners like the Webbs, and Quaker reformists like Booth and Rountree found and documented enough wrongs in the late Victorian Poor Law to successfully pave the way first for the Liberal Reforms 1906-1911, and eventually to Labour Reforms 1945-48 which created social security, a national health service, free education and public housing.

As the state moved in, so the role of charity became more obscure. Could a service that the state provides be charitable? Was contemporary charity more to do with the nature of the organisation carrying out an activity than with the nature of the activity itself?

The four "heads of charity" established by McNaughton remained as a definition of charity. However, it was now the state that bore responsibility for poverty, education and health. Only the promotion of religion remained as a largely private endeavour.

To add to the confusion, the state began to set up and fund charities directly. After the Second World War, several "councils for..." were established to meet the additional needs of those (including many war veterans) with various types of disability. These have since become household names in the charity sector, and included Councils for:

- o   The disabled
- o   The blind
- o   The deaf
- o   The mentally infirm (Mind and Mencap today)

The nature of these bodies was further complicated by the development of several QUANGOs[2] such as Remploy, which also relied on state funding and also carried out work that had previously been viewed as charitable.

Throughout the post war years, the state gradually expanded its influence over charities, creating organisations such as The Marriage Guidance Council (now Relate) in an effort to prevent changes to the divorce laws in 1969 resulting in a stampede to the courts.

A perverse consequence of the state funding of charities has been an arms race in executive pay that has gradually served to undermine the supposed voluntary nature of charity. At the time of writing there is a public debate around whether the Trustees of charities should also be paid. While 75 percent of the public are opposed to this proposals, within the political class, and among the charity sector there is greater support for payment where trustees are in charge of big multi-million-pound organisations.

---

[2] Quasi-Autonomous Non-Government Organisations – essentially organisations that carry out government's administrative functions at arm's length from Ministerial control. Most often, QUANGOs are governed by boards of directors with particular technical expertise, appointed by the Minister in charge of the government department that oversees/funds them.

By the late 1990s, the McNaughton definition of charity had worn thin. Where did animal rescue charities fit within health, education, poverty or religion? What about the growing number of environmental groups that sought the benefits of charitable status?

In order to answer these questions, the Charities Act 2006 set out 12 heads of charity:

1. the prevention or relief of poverty
2. the advancement of education
3. the advancement of religion
4. the advancement of health or the saving of lives
5. the advancement of citizenship or community development
6. the advancement of the arts, culture, heritage or science
7. the advancement of amateur sport
8. the advancement of human rights, conflict resolution or reconciliation or the promotion of religious or racial harmony or equality and diversity
9. the advancement of environmental protection or improvement
10. the relief of those in need by reason of youth, age, ill-health, disability, financial hardship or other disadvantage
11. the advancement of animal welfare
12. the promotion of the efficiency of the armed forces of the Crown, or of the efficiency of the police, fire and rescue services or ambulance services.

The 2006 Act also introduced clauses to require that to qualify as a charity, an organisation must be established solely for charitable purposes and it must pass a public benefit test. Unfortunately, neither of these clauses was properly defined, creating an Alice in Wonderland situation in which "charity" means anything that the government of the day wants it to mean!

Although the Con-Dem government that entered office in May 2010 had talked about reforming charity law, in practice they maintained the 2006 provisions. A new Charities Act 2011 merely consolidated several pieces of pre-existing law. In terms of reform, in the end the government decided to kick the whole issue into the long grass by (in the usual British manner) appointing a conservative peer (Lord Hodgson) to conduct a review of the Charities Act 2006. As of October 2013, there are no plans for further legislation.

In practice, it has been left to an increasingly under-resourced Charity Commission to bring test cases before the courts so that civil law would ultimately decide what constituted "public benefit" and "charitable purpose" across what has become a vast tract of civil society. However, the Charity Commission lacks the resources to take public interest cases through the courts. So, for the time being, the legal meaning of "charity" will remain unclear.

Lack of regulation

Becoming registered as a charity does not indicate an organisation has passed a quality threshold. It merely means that the organisation meets the statutory criteria for registration. Nonetheless, registration is seen by many donors as a 'kitemark' that increases their confidence in, and likelihood of, giving to a charity. The Commission's regulatory activity is important in upholding the public's confidence and trust in charities generally[3].

According to the Charity Commission, at the end of December 2013 there were 163,709[4] charities in England and Wales[5]:

o 68,658 (41.9%) with an income less than £10,000 accounting for just 0.4% of charity income
o 54,593 (33.3 %) with £10,000 to £100,000 accounting for 3.1% of charity income
o 20,625 (12.6 %) with £100,000 to £500,000 accounting for 7.4% of charity income
o 8,146 (5.0 %) with £500,000 to £5 million accounting for 20.1% of charity income
o 1,918 (1.2 %) with more than £5 million accounting for 69.0% of charity income.

---

[3] *The regulatory effectiveness of the Charity Commission.* National Audit Office, November 2013.
[4] This figure mainly refers to registered charities. According to the Public Administration Committee, there may be more than 350,000 charitable organisations (most very small) working in the UK.
[5] charitycommission.gov.uk/about-charities/sector-facts-and-figures

There were an additional 9,769 (6.0%) of charities whose income was not known to the Charity Commission.

The number of registered charities in England and Wales reached a high point of 169,297 on the eve of the banking crash in 2007. Numbers fell sharply to 160,515 in 2009 as a result of closures and mergers, before rising gradually again.

Total charity income has risen steadily from £23.74bn in 1999 to £61.43bn in 2013.

Over the same period, the top 1% of charities has seen their share of total charity income rise steadily from 42.9% in 1999 to 58.4% in 2013.

Almost all organisations or associations in England and Wales with an income of £5,000 are required to register as charities unless they are among a small number of exempt categories or unless they have another legal structure such as a limited company or a community interest company.

However, *registration with* the Charity Commission does not mean *regulation by* the Charity Commission. Although in law all charities are regulated by the Charity Commission, in practice, most of the charity sector is like the Wild West. The Charity Commission lacks the resources to carry out many proactive "visits" to charities, and most of those that are carried out fall far short of the kind of inspection and audit that most members of the public would expect.

Organisations with an income greater than £500,000 are subject to a full, independent audit. These will be conducted by one or more Chartered Accountants who risk being struck off in the event of their not accurately reporting on charities' activities. Unsurprisingly, levels of fraud and mismanagement among the 10,000 charities in this category are significantly lower than are found among the other 153,600 or so registered charities.

Organisations with incomes between £25,000 and £500,000 must post their accounts and annual report to the Charity Commission. The accounts must also be "scrutinised" by an "independent examiner"[6]. Unfortunately, this process can leave members of the public with the false sense that some form of formal audit has been carried out. In practice, scrutiny falls far short of an audit, with the independent examiner merely declaring that the statement of income and expenditure in the accounts matches the pattern of income and expenditure in the bank statements, and that some form of receipt is available for each donation and payment. Were an unscrupulous charity manager to choose simply to forge receipts and invoices, there is nothing in the independent examination process to expose this. Nor is there anything within the process to guarantee that donors' money was spent on the activities promised or that the declared "charitable activities" were, indeed, charitable.

---

[6] In many cases this will be an accountant, but there is no legal obligation to pay an accountant. Someone who works or is retired from other finance professions such as banking may also act as an independent examiner.

Organisations with incomes of less than £25,000 are not even required to post their annual accounts and annual report[7], so there is no way members of the public can access these records to see whether these bodies have spent their donors' money on the activities that they promised.

In practice, the Charity Commission relies on reports from whistle-blowers, donors, beneficiaries and concerned members of the public to draw attention to fraud and mismanagement within charities. Sadly, the experience of many of those who raise concerns about charities is either to find themselves ignored, or to discover that even though the Charity Commission has identified possible fraud or serious misconduct, they have left it to the charity's trustees (i.e., the very people who allowed the misconduct to occur) to deal with the issue:

> "The Commission's approach to charities is too trusting. It has frequently relied on assurances from trustees that they have taken action, or would take action to address its concerns, rather than checking directly whether trustees had actually taken the required action"[8].

Unfortunately, in the last 20 years, the Charity

---

[7] Those charities that are also limited companies are required to post abbreviated accounts to Companies House, however, these are only available on payment of a fee.

[8] Committee of Public Accounts, The Charity Commission, Forty-second Report of Session 2013–14

Commission has deliberately abrogated their key role as a policeman regulating charities on behalf of donors, beneficiaries and the public at large. As the National Audit Office notes:

> "Our four previous reports on the Commission's performance, over the past 26 years, repeatedly identified concerns about the Commission's follow-up of regulatory concerns, use of its powers, management of resources, the relevance of its performance targets, and use of information"[9].

In the 1990s, the Charity Commission was widely feared among charity trustees and senior staff because of the sanctions that could (and most probably would) be applied if you did things wrong. This environment (although not perfect) created a high degree of self-policing across charities, allowing the Charity Commission to focus limited resources on investigating the most serious cases of misconduct.

By the mid-2000s, the Charity Commission had lost sight of who it was they were regulating on behalf of (i.e. donors, beneficiaries and the wider public). Rather, they chose to become the "charities' friend". Instead of stamping on charities that broke the rules, they would offer "guidance and support" to the trustees and managers to help them get back on track. Rather like a policeman who thinks he will be popular if he turns a

[9] National Audit Office, The regulatory effectiveness of the Charity Commission, HC 813 Session 2013-14 4 December 2013

blind eye to low-level crime, what the Charity Commission succeeded in creating was a free-for-all. Self-policing among charities broke down as fraudsters and chancers saw that in practice there was no de facto regulation for the majority of charities.

Although the incidence of fraud and misconduct in the running of charities has risen remorselessly with the relaxation of regulation, this is but one element of what has been allowed to go wrong. In addition, the Charity Commission chose to actively encourage charities to participate in areas of public life where they had previously feared to tread. Most obviously, the Charity Commission actively encouraged charities to enter the political arena. Throughout history, charity and politics have been regarded as inconsistent. The reasons for this are neatly summed up in a 1981 High Court judgement. Justice Slade held that[10]:

> "The court will not regard as charitable a trust of which a main object is to procure an alteration of the law of the United Kingdom for one or both of two reasons: first, the court will ordinarily have no sufficient means of judging as a matter of evidence whether the proposed change will or will not be for the public benefit. Secondly, even if the evidence suffices to enable it to form a prima facie opinion that a change in the law is desirable, it must still decide the case on the principle that the law is right as it stands, since to do otherwise would usurp the

[10] McGovern v AG 1981 3 All ER 49, HC

functions of the legislature".

In other words, just because you (and/or the charity you work for) say that a particular change in law or practice will have a charitable benefit does not make the statement true. And even if it were true, it is for Parliament rather than judges or charities to determine what changes are necessary.

Despite this, by the early 2000s, the Charity Commission was actually ahead of the majority of charities (which expressed considerable reluctance to engage in the political process), encouraging and supporting them to become involved in the political arena. As we shall see, far from enhancing the reputation of charities, active engagement in the political process has created a growing climate of mistrust in charities. Rather than acting in the public interest, far too many charities are acting on behalf of vested interests – often to the detriment of their beneficiaries and of the public good.

Belatedly, and largely as a result of funding cuts, the Charity Commission has been forced to review its activities. This has led to the promise that more attention will be given to policing charities. In 2012, the new Chairman of the Charity Commission warned:

> "… that he would step in to curb their political campaigning if they 'overstepped the mark', and act as a 'policeman' if necessary. He also criticised the way many charities have become so

'dependent' on Government grants that some have even stopped fund-raising altogether"[11].

Faced with severe budget cuts, the Charity Commission has also made clear that the provision of guidance and support (beyond the general guidance posted on the Charity Commission website) is something that charities will now have to find (and where necessary purchase) for themselves.

However, if the Charity Commission is to restore the self-policing that used to occur within charities, it will need to take a firm but fair approach to imposing appropriate penalties on trustees and managers where misconduct has occurred. In the end, as is the case with police officers, being popular is not the point – being respected is the aim. To achieve respect, you have to impose the rules properly and equitably:

> "… by seeking to be an advice service to charities, the Commission also risks a conflict of interest: it cannot simultaneously maintain public trust in the charitable sector while also acting as a champion of charities and the charitable sector. The latter should be, as the Commission and Lord Hodgson have recommended, a role for the sector's umbrella bodies and not its regulator.[12]"

---

[11] Daily Telegraph. 10 December 2012.

[12] House of Commons, 21 May 2013

The measure of successful regulation should be that charity managers and trustees view the Charity Commission with the same sense of trepidation with which a speeding driver views a traffic police car in the rear view mirror – a feeling that causes the majority of us to drive safely and within the speed limit.

The National Audit Office concluded that:

> "The Commission is not regulating charities effectively. It does important and necessary work and its independent status is highly valued, but it does not do enough to identify and tackle abuse of charitable status. It uses its information poorly to assess risk and often relies solely on trustees' assurances. Where it does identify concerns in charities, it makes little use of its powers and fails to take tough action in some of the most serious cases. This undermines the Commission's ability to meet its statutory objective to increase public trust and confidence in charities"[13].

In future, the Charity Commission will need to adopt and firmly stick to one of two common approaches to regulation. It could create an inspection regime similar to that used in education or social care, so that every charity understands that if they engage in mismanagement or fraud, they will be caught. Alternatively, it could adopt a system similar to that used in television licensing in

[13] National Audit Office, The regulatory effectiveness of the Charity Commission, HC 813 Session 2013-14 4 December 2013

which, while the odds of getting caught may be low, the penalties are high[14]. Ideally, of course, the Charity Commission would adopt both approaches in order to maintain public trust. It might be possible, for example, for the Charity Commission to set up an audit and investigation unit funded, at least in part, by major donors (including the state) to ensure that charitable funds are being spent properly. But for now, weak (or de facto non-existent) regulation is helping to fuel vested interests, fraud, crime and corruption.

---

[14] The maximum penalty for non-payment is a fine of £1,000. Failure or inability to pay will often result in imprisonment.

Paid Employees

According to the UK Government's Labour Force Survey 2012, more than 800,000 people are now employed in the "voluntary sector" – accounting for around 3 percent of the UK workforce. This is an increase of just under 250,000 since 2002, and is largely explained by the big charities entering into contracts to deliver public services as a response to cuts in direct government funding of charities.

At the time of writing there is public concern about the high levels of CEO salaries in the charitable sector. The Daily Telegraph[15] has highlighted 30 charity CEOs with salaries of more than £100,000, while The Guardian[16] has produced a table showing CEO salaries of more than £30,000 for a range of national charities. The Charity Commission has warned the trustees of these leading charities that they need to be able to justify any pay awards they make. Against this, umbrella organisations such as the Association of Charity Chief Executives (ACEVO) have argued that charity CEO salaries are modest in comparison to the scale of the work that CEOs oversee.

More worrying than the high levels of CEO remuneration is the growing disparity between pay at the top of charities and the pay of those who deliver charity services.

[15] www.telegraph.co.uk/news/politics/10224104/30-charity-chiefs - paid- more-than-100000
[16] society.theguardian.com/salarysurvey/table/0,,1043285,00

Charities account for 36 percent of all zero hours contracts – twice as many as the private sector. This is often in direct contradiction of the causes that many of these charities claim to promote. For example, several major mental health charities employ staff on zero hours contracts despite berating other employers on the negative effects on mental health of such poor employment terms and conditions.

The terms of the debate – not least by groups like ACEVO – seek to give the impression that the payment of staff within the charity sector is normal. But this is far from the truth. As we have seen, just 5.2 percent of charities with annual incomes above £500,000 account for more than 75 percent of the more than £62 billion raised annually by charities in England and Wales. Voluntary sector employment is concentrated in this small proportion of the sector.

In fact, paying staff remains the exception rather than the rule. And this should prompt us to ask more fundamental questions about charity pay:

o Should charities be allowed to have paid employees at all? and
o What are the consequences for charities when they do?

At the heart of charity is the notion of voluntarism. That is, individuals voluntarily donate their time (volunteers) and/or money (donors) via a body governed by volunteers (trustees) for the sole benefit of those less fortunate (beneficiaries) than they are. In this model – which represents the way in which the vast majority of charities operate – the only people who are supposed to benefit from charity are those recognised in the aims and objects as beneficiaries (e.g. children, poor people, older people, etc).

Donors, trustees and volunteers are reimbursed only through expenses payments (trustees and volunteers) or tax relief (donors). They may also benefit from a sense of personal wellbeing and virtue that often accompanies actions that help others.

Trustees are forbidden by law from benefiting financially precisely because this would add a new vested interest that would distort the operation of the model. However, at the time of writing, many larger charities have called for a change in the law to allow for the payment of trustees because they believe that salaries will attract people with the skills required to manage and oversee what have become multi-million pound national and multi-national businesses.

This is a very similar debate to those around the payment of Members of Parliament and, more recently, the payment of local councillors. In each case, payment is intended to resolve the problems caused by the inability of the public's unpaid representatives to exercise strategic control of the paid professional staff. However, in each of these cases, payment has simply created a new vested interest that is often in its own way as opposed to the public interest as are the interests of paid professionals.

There is an equally plausible argument in the case of the overwhelming majority of charities that the employment of paid staff should be prohibited. The problem is that once a charity enters into an employment relationship with paid staff, it must comply with the same swathe of employment law and regulation faced (and oft complained about) by private businesses. Any decisions an employing charity makes can no longer be based solely on the evolving needs of its beneficiaries, but must first and foremost protect the employment and terms and conditions of the paid employees.

Once professional staff are employed, this problem deepens. Whereas the paid staff – often employed for their expertise – become intimately involved in the management and operation of the charity on a daily basis, the voluntary trustees often come together just once a month (sometimes less often) to oversee the operation of the charity. As the relationship between paid employees and volunteer trustees develops, so the trustees become increasingly dependent upon the advice of paid employees to inform their decision making. Indeed, one of the key arguments made in favour of paying the trustees of large charities is precisely to redress this imbalance.

In order to protect or improve their own and their colleagues' employment and conditions, senior staff may begin to engage in a range of morally dubious activities such as:

- o Selling their charity's reputation to the highest bidder
- o Exaggerating and fabricating research findings to make a case for their cause
- o Shifting their charity's aims and objects (often unlawfully) to avoid redundancy
- o Engaging in business and employment practices that are at odds with their aims and objects
- o Investing in the very evils (e.g. weapons, pollution, tobacco, etc) that they claim to be combatting.

I will deal with each of these in turn in later chapters. Suffice to say at this point that these are all activities that would not be engaged in by entirely voluntary charities, but have become the stock in trade among the biggest charities.

Nor are these practices the result of "a few bad apples". Rather, these are the inevitable consequences of the need to support employment within a globalised market economy. For example, the BBC[17] has raised questions about the relationship between the charity Save the Children and its sponsor, British Gas. Over a ten-year period, Save the Children received £1.5 million from British Gas. According to the BBC, during that period the charity toned down its messages about the effects of fuel price rises on child poverty so as not to risk the income from sponsorship. Although the charity denies that it would halt a campaign or tone down its message for fear of losing a sponsor, the BBC says that it has internal e-mails that show that the charity continued to tone down

[17] www.bbc.co.uk/news/uk-25273024

its message in an attempt to win corporate sponsorship from another big energy company, EDF.

Nor does the employment of staff only cause charities to pull their punches for fear of alienating sponsors and potential sponsors. Consider the case of Age UK – the charity formed out of the merger of Age Concern and Help the Aged. The charity has an income of £159 million, and employs more than 2,200 staff including 44 who have salaries above £60,000 (8 of whom have salaries above £100,000). Like many large charities, Age UK has inherited a large pension deficit from defined benefit schemes run by each of the charities that merged to become Age UK. The charity has an income of more than £1.6 million from corporate sponsorship and events. Worryingly, the charity has been accused of putting the needs of some of its corporate sponsors over those of its beneficiaries. For example, according to the Daily Telegraph[18], the charity has been advising beneficiaries with mobility problems to contact one of their sponsors, Quingo (a company that uses high-pressure sales techniques to encourage elderly people to buy expensive mobility scooters). According to The Independent[19] Age UK also passed beneficiaries' details to Nursing Homes Fees Agency – which "mis-sold" (i.e. fraudulently sold) £10.5 billion of inappropriate investments to thousands of pensioners.

[18] www.telegraph.co.uk/finance/newsbysector/retailandconsumer / 10348383/Age-UK-launches-investigation-into-scooter-firm-that-pressurises-elderly-people

[19] www.independent.co.uk/money/spend-save/age-charity- profited -from-hsbc-scandal-6273291

It is not that charities deliberately set out to put the needs of employees above those of beneficiaries. However, the raft of employment law and regulation that all but the smallest organisations must comply with is far more tightly enforced – and the potential penalties for infringement are far greater – than the limp regulatory system that the Charity Commission operates on behalf of beneficiaries and donors. Inevitably, this creates pressure to put the needs of paid staff above all else. Once staff are employed, the pressure is on to maintain income streams, avoid pension deficits and prevent what can be costly redundancy processes. This, in turn, creates significant pressure to shift objectives, modify campaigning messages, and to operate in the interests of funders, even when these are in conflict with the needs of charities' beneficiaries or the appeals made to individual donors.

While acknowledging that we are unlikely to see any change to charities' ability to employ people directly, it is important to understand that employment inevitably has negative outcomes for beneficiaries, and can ultimately damage the reputation of both individual charities and the sector. A sensible half-way house would be to alter the terms under which charities engage employees.

Many of the larger charities have answered these issues (albeit unfairly) in relation to junior staff through the use of zero-hours contracts that effectively transfer the burden of employment law and regulation onto the shoulders of the employees. A fairer approach would be to encourage the use of paid consultancies (which also carry the burden of employment law) where charities' work can be contracted-out. Where functions cannot be conducted by external consultants, charities should, at the very least, do away with permanent full-time contracts in favour of short-term contracts tied to clear performance measurements and penalty clauses. This is particularly important where senior employees seek six-figure salaries, where performance should be a key issue. After all, a six-figure salary in the charity sector can only be justified if it results in major improvements for beneficiaries.

Far from paying a new self-interest group of remunerated trustees to oversee increasingly bloated senior managers, this, too, would see some of the burden of employment law and regulation transferred from the charity to the senior employee – leaving the trustees primarily concerned with charity regulation.

Crime and Corruption

In 2001, the first Welsh Assembly Government launched its flagship policy aimed at tackling poverty and the many social ills that result from it. Public funds were to be used to co-produce poverty reduction through a series of partnerships with local communities in the 180 most deprived areas of Wales. In practice, the "Communities First" programme was to be delivered through state-created and state-funded charities managed by suitably trained residents of the communities they served.

Initially, the charities were developed and supported by their local authority, which oversaw the recruitment and training of trustees, together with appropriate management and reporting. However, the aim was always to allow these charities to become independent bodies – not least because this would allow them to find additional funding over and above that provided by the state.

In most cases, the Communities First charities found themselves propelled into the top tier of UK charities thanks to grants of more than £500,000 from the Welsh Assembly Government. This meant that they were subject to the very highest levels of charity regulation, reporting and audit.

In 2011, the Welsh Government was obliged to put the whole Communities First programme on hold pending the outcome of inquiries and criminal proceedings that suggested that fraud, mismanagement and poor practice were rife.

At the centre of this storm was Plas Madoc Communities First (PMCF), the charity set up to serve the 1,800 residents of the Plas Madoc estate on the outskirts of Wrexham in northeast Wales.

Within the Welsh third sector, there had been widespread rumours about corruption and fraud within PMCF. I personally encountered this in the summer of 2008, during a break at a conference I was attending. Some delegates who had worked with PMCF, and had witnessed fraudulent activity had asked me about the way charities were regulated, and about how best to raise their concerns.

It was to be another three years before the public began to realise the extent of the fraud and corruption that had taken place.

In December 2011, PMCF chief executive officer Miriam Beard was jailed for 32 months after admitting to nine counts of fraud involving the theft of £51,000 of the charity's funds. Her son received a 12 month suspended sentence for his part in the fraud, and was ordered to repay £15,000 to the charity.

So far as the public were concerned, that was that. But the criminal proceedings against the PMCF CEO and her son were just the tip of the iceberg. Hidden from public view was a culture of lower grade corruption and mismanagement that pervaded the charity.

A Wales Audit Office report[20] into the activities within the charity found a catalogue of "perks" provided to or taken by members of staff and their relatives, apparently without the knowledge or approval of the charity's trustees. These included:

o Awarding contracts to family members without going through an appropriate tendering process
o Family members receiving payments of several thousand pounds for mobile phones and petrol with no evidence of these being used while working for the charity
o Payment of staff members' mobile phone bills – again running to thousands of pounds (the Finance Officer's two daughters each receiving more than £3,000 a year)
o Staff (particularly the CEO) abuse of petrol allowances, and a lack of documentation and reconciliation of petrol expenses claims
o The provision of interest-free loans to staff, without appropriate systems for guaranteeing that these would be repaid
o Misuse of petty cash accounts – particularly to launder funds from income-generating activities so that these would not have to go through the charity's accounts
o Unlawful payments to a board member of more than £10,000
o The payment of staff parking fines

[20] www.wao.gov.uk/publication/plas-madoc-communities-first

- Paying £2,667 of the charity's funds for a staff Christmas party
- Using petty cash to buy various (wedding, birthday, etc) presents for staff.

No doubt, had the above not been serious enough, the Audit would have also uncovered the run of the mill pilfering of biros, notepads, computer software and hardware, etc. that goes on to some degree within almost every organisation.

However, the issue here is not that there are criminally minded people at large who will happily line their own pockets even at the expense of some of the poorest people in society. Given the behaviour of bankers, expenses-fiddling MPs, phone hacking journalists, greed-driven energy companies, and all the other expressions of self-interest that plague modern Britain, we really should not be surprised that the same types of corruption and mismanagement occur in the charity sector. As with banking, the behaviour of MPs, the activities of newspaper editors, etc, the key issue here is the failure of oversight and regulation.

PMCF was not a small, local charity with an annual income of less than £5,000 operated by a handful of amateurs, each giving up a few hours a month for a good cause. PMCF had an annual income of more than three-quarters of a million pounds. A large part of this was public funding, with additional funds coming from major funding bodies such as the Big Lottery and the Arts

Council.

PMCF's board of trustees should have been a model of good practice. They were not. The Welsh Audit Office commented that:

> "The Board within PMCF has not been providing the necessary strategic direction and leadership for the organisation and they have failed to undertake an appropriate scrutiny of the work of its paid officials. Managers and Board Members do not understand their stewardship responsibilities and our findings have shown that there appears to have been little regard for the Standards of Public Life or achieving Value for Money with public funds. A significant change of culture within the organisation is required, particularly as it was concerning to note that the people interviewed during the course of our review continually commented on the 'Culture of Generosity' that has been created for staff within PMCF. This generosity within PMCF has, in our view, been at the detriment of those individuals in the local community who were meant to benefit from the public funds allocated to the Communities First programme".

All charities with an income of more than £500,000 are subject to a full independent audit. This is meant to provide a first line of defence against fraud and mismanagement. Independent auditors have a duty to raise any concerns they uncover and to report these to the relevant authorities. However, in the case of PMCF, the external auditor chose only to report concerns about the charity's financial controls in a letter to the board of trustees (sent via the Finance Officer). Concerns were not raised with the Charity Commission, HMRC, the Welsh Assembly Government or any of the other funding bodies.

Whatever else the PMCF case tells us, it confirms that the current gold standard regulation of charities in England and Wales fails to prevent widespread and large scale fraud, criminality and mismanagement.

Smaller charities – those with incomes between £25,000 and £500,000 – need only provide an "independent examiners' review" of their accounts. This falls far short of an independent audit, and is even less likely to result in concerns being raised with regulators or funders. Charities with incomes below £25,000 are not subject to independent scrutiny of any kind.

The question this must raise is that if a charity as well-supported and well-funded as PMCF is subject to such poor management and oversight, what is the state of management and oversight in the wider charity sector?

When a complaint against PMCF was made to the Welsh Assembly Government by a worker and a trustee of PMCF, the complainants were told to sort it out with PMCF themselves! In fact, this "sort it out amongst yourselves" approach is an all too common line taken by government departments and the Charity Commission in response to public complaints. With the exception of a handful of fashionable complaints (such as those involving money laundering or potential links with terrorist bodies), regulators have tended to leave complaints to the trustees of the charities concerned – even when (as was the case with PMCF) the complaints are made by one or more of the trustees themselves.

Most often, trustees and other whistle blowers who find themselves in this position simply walk away. Indeed, giving evidence to the Welsh Government following the PMCF scandal, Wales Council for Voluntary Action argued that much more rigorous action needed to be taken when the trustees of charities resign, as this is often the only step left to them to avoid personal liability for the fraud and/or mismanagement that is taking place.

And again, we are bound to ask, if the regulators do not act on complaints made against large, publicly funded charities like PMCF, what happens in the rest of the sector?

Facing questions from the Parliamentary Public Accounts Committee in March 2013, chair of the Charity Commission William Shawcross blithely stated that "99% of charities are good, decent and proper". We have of course seen this "one bad apple" line trotted out by a range of regulators in relation to such diverse areas as phone-hacking by newspapers, MPs expenses, the police after Hillsborough and the murder of Steven Lawrence, banking, etc. But the sad truth is that more often than not, fraud and mismanagement turn out to be institutional failings – usually exacerbated by so-called "light touch regulation". The fact is that the Charity Commission does not know how many charities are engaged in fraud and mismanagement because they lack the resources and the inclination to investigate even when charity trustees and/or staff come forward to blow the whistle.

You may choose to follow the "one bad apple" line by suggesting I am making too much of the PMCF case. However, my reasons for choosing to use it as an example are only that:

o Criminal proceedings have been settled, so there are no longer issues about publishing information that could prejudice a trial
o The investigation conducted by the Welsh Audit Office picked up important governance issues that would not have been obvious to a member of the public reading press coverage of the criminal case
o I know several of the people who first raised complaints about PMCF.

I could, for example, have given the example of AWEMA – another large, publicly funded Welsh charity where there are allegations of fraud and mismanagement involving millions of pounds of public funding. However, since charges have been brought against that charity's former CEO, and the case is yet to be heard, this would be more difficult to report on. Nevertheless, I would recommend that you refer to the Wales Online website, and look at Chief reporter Martin Shipton's[21] coverage of a host of charity and public funding scandals of one kind or another that have surfaced in recent years.

Nor are such scandals limited to Wales. According to the National Fraud Authority, fraud in the charity sector amounts to more than £1.3 billion every year. This figure may underestimate borderline issues such as trustees benefiting by receiving pay from their charity, trustees and/or senior staff employing or granting contracts to family members, and all of those other apparently minor practices like paying personal phone and petrol costs uncovered at PMCF.

The truth is that the trust that the public has given to charities has blinded us to the fact that people who work in and who manage charities are no different to the people who work in banking, journalism, politics, policing and public utilities. That is, while most are entirely upstanding and trustworthy, a damaging minority are not.

Unfortunately, as with all scandals, what we find is that regulation has been particularly lax. And this is not simply about the passivity of the Charity Commission. In practice, donors must take their share of the blame too. In the case of PMCF, major donors like the Big Lottery and the Welsh Government failed to ensure that a charity they were providing funds to was fit for purpose. Like so many members of the public, they seem to have assumed that

[21] www.walesonline.co.uk/authors/martin-shipton

charity registration is sufficient to guarantee probity – it is not.

All donors have a duty to ask searching questions about the charities they fund. And bigger funders – such as the Welsh Government – have a duty to protect public funds and to act on complaints they receive from whistle blowers. It is a duty that they too often renege on.

Tax Avoidance and Evasion

In the charity sector you will often hear people say, "Charities don't pay tax". I have even encountered accountants (who should know better) asserting this. In practice, there may be a kernel of truth within the myth, but this owes more to HMRC deciding not to pay much attention to charities than it does to tax law.

In law, charities are only exempt from tax *on their charitable activities* and only then if tax relief could not be seen as providing a competitive advantage that might distort EU trade. There is no "blank cheque" exemption that allows charities to trade or to run public services without having to pay the same rates of tax as any other form of organisation that engages in these activities.

It is worth considering why society affords charities tax reliefs that other types of organisation do not enjoy.

Insofar as charity is a voluntary activity that is conducted for public benefit, it has attracted a series of privileges that are not available to private enterprises or public authorities. However, as we have seen, the drive to be "business-like" has blurred the distinctions between these other activities to the point where it is difficult to argue the case for tax and business rates relief simply on the basis of an organisation's legal status. What, for example, is the difference between a charity and a commercial business that provides contracted public social care services? In such a case, doesn't tax relief provide the charity with an unfair (and possibly unlawful) state subsidy? On a smaller scale, why should a charity shop whose income pays for the six-figure salary of the CEO enjoy business rates relief while the corner shop that (barely) pays the five-figure income of its proprietor must pay the full amount?

As the reasons behind charity tax privileges fade into history, and in the face of very lax regulation, we are witnessing a series of tax scandals that must, ultimately, lead to a re-thinking of charity tax law. For example, in 2009 the Cup Trust was set up ostensibly to benefit needy children and young people. By 2011 it had raised £176 million from its wealthy donors, but had distributed just £55,000 to beneficiaries. There was more than a suspicion that the Cup Trust was a tax avoidance scheme, and that its operation might constitute tax fraud.

The scheme operated by using an offshore bank loan to buy £1m gilts, which were then sold to investors (who had paid a nominal fee to join the scheme). The Cup Trust then donated about £500 to charity on the investors' behalf and the investors would sell the gilts and "donate" the money to the Cup Trust. This allowed them to claim between £250,000 and £375,000 (depending on their tax rate) in Gift Aid Relief. The Cup Trust then used the donation to repay the loan. But charities could only benefit from the Cup Trust scheme if HMRC approved it, and agreed to pay Gift Aid on the "donations" made by the scheme's tax avoiding backers. That is, indirectly, the taxpayer would be the only one actually making a contribution to charity.

Bizarrely, at the time of writing, it appears that there is nothing unlawful about schemes like the Cup Trust. The Parliamentary Public Accounts Committee says it is aware of at least 50 similar schemes waiting for HMRC to rule whether they are eligible for Gift Aid. According to the Charity Commission, if HMRC pays the Gift Aid, then the schemes will qualify as charitable.

The Cup Trust scandal is merely the tip of a very big iceberg of charity tax avoidance and tax fraud. The scandal's rise to prominence probably reflects a broader public concern about large corporations and wealthy individuals finding elaborate ways of avoiding paying their fair share while the majority go through the pain of austerity cuts and wage freezes. As accountancy journalist Philip Fisher says[22]:

> "While we all know that charity begins at home, using the wrapper of an organisation theoretically designed to help those in need as a means to obtain tax relief does sound very much closer to fraud than even tax evasion, let alone avoidance.

> "Certainly, to the man in the street, this will sound exactly like another fraud perpetrated with the aid of members of the tax industry i.e. the accounting or legal professions, which is likely to leave all of us

[22] Philip Fisher. *Morality Is Back on the Agenda - Forget Tax Evasion, Surely This Is Fraud?* Accounting Web. 4 December 2013

feeling embarrassed even though 99% would not dream of becoming involved in such activities".

Less spectacular tax dodging occurs up and down the land, day in, day out. Since 2008, under-occupancy in the commercial rented sector – particularly in high street shops – has led landlords to seek a means of avoiding paying business rates on their empty properties. Ideally, they should be lowering their rents in order to make their premises viable for the new businesses that would revitalise our high streets. However, charities enjoy a mandatory relief of 80 percent of business rates, and many also qualify for the additional discretionary 20 percent relief provided by local authorities. This has created a perverse situation in which private landlords are better off *giving* rent-free accommodation to charities than competing to *rent* premises to small businesses. Indeed, in many cases the savings on business rates are so great that landlords have even paid the remaining 20 percent of business rates on behalf of the charity as this still leaves them better off.

In the most fraudulent cases, charities have done nothing more than put their name on a lease. In effect the building remains empty, but business rates are avoided. But even where charities do enjoy free access to commercial premises which they then use either as an office or a trading space, this serves to limit supply and thereby drive up the costs of the remaining commercial property that might otherwise be available to new and small businesses.

In recent years there has been growing concern about some charity shop and café chains using their tax and business rates reliefs to gain an unfair advantage over potential competitors. This concern is probably overstated – large supermarkets and out-of-town retail parks are a much greater threat to small shops than charity shops will ever be. However, these concerns do raise questions about the way tax and business rates reliefs are operated. For example, should the split between mandatory and discretionary business rates relief be altered? One option under consideration in Wales is to bring in a 50/50 split, allowing local authorities to incentivise those charities that operate within the local community while removing some of the relief from large chains who use their income to fund head offices in Cardiff or London.

On the other side of the debate, there is clearly a need to level the playing field for small businesses and social enterprises. At present there are discretionary temporary reliefs for these organisations. However, over time we are likely to move to a regime in which they too enjoy much greater permanent business rates relief, while higher rates are imposed on large commercial and retail premises.

As the state shifts the funding that it has provided to charity from grants to public service contracts, so the current system of tax privileges becomes even more questionable. The advantage to the state of engaging charity in the provision of public services is that this helps to drive down the price. Charities often use their tax exemption to undercut commercial organisations that might otherwise win government contracts. Charities are also much better able to use the free labour of volunteers to deliver services that would otherwise have to be carried out by paid employees. These advantages to the state are no doubt one of the reasons why HMRC has chosen to look the other way when it comes to assessing the tax liabilities of charities. It is far from clear that the charities that deliver public services could make the case that all of these activities are charitable. And if the activities are not charitable, then these charities should be paying their share of tax.

Moreover, the involvement of charities in public service delivery is beginning to have negative consequences. Charities have been forced to adopt zero-hours contracts and to flout the Minimum Wage in order to secure the contracts that they now need in order to survive. Charities now use twice as many zero-hours contracts as private firms. Several have also been caught exploiting the unpaid labour of people who are supposed to be their beneficiaries through engagement with several government workfare schemes. This raises the question as to whether such charities should enjoy tax and business rate privileges to enable them to behave in this way.

For the majority of charities, these issues are only a problem for the unwary – where tax evaders and tax fraudsters seek to dupe them into participating in or lending their names to tax and business rates dodging schemes. But for the minority of big super-charities these issues are likely to become a problem in the near future.

While the government's 2012 attempt to limit Gift Aid to the higher of either £50,000 or 25 percent of income was dropped, it signals a shift away from an automatic assumption that charity and charitable donations should be tax free. Add in the concerns about schemes like the Cup Trust, and abuse of business rates relief, and you begin to see a political shift toward more nuanced tax reliefs for charities.

Political Campaigning

Currently, there is debate around the campaigning activities of charities, with the government pushing through anti-lobbying legislation to silence charities in the run up to general elections. These measures are over the top – not least because proper regulation by the Charity Commission using existing powers could achieve similar results. However, charity campaigning is generally anti-democratic insofar as it seeks to empower an increasingly authoritarian state to regulate the behaviour of the people. This being the case, we need to be very clear about the way charities are allowed to engage with the political process.

The role of charities in public debate legitimates a modern version of the "corporatist state". In a corporatist political system, the role of the state is to balance and adjudicate the competing claims and needs of a range of bodies – in Mussolini's original formulation of this type of system balance was largely between capital and labour (although always ultimately favouring capital). In contemporary Britain, corporatism extends beyond the traditional trades unions and employers organisations to encompass professions, educational establishments, state departments (particularly those involved in "security") and charities.

In a functioning democracy, the disinterested "will of the people" would take precedence in all matters. However, almost all charities elevate their particular "corporate" interest above the public interest. For example, a cancer charity will make the case for an expensive new treatment to be provided irrespective of the cost to the public purse and without concern for the other people whose services will have to be cut if the new treatment is to be funded. Similarly, local environmental groups will campaign against new strategic transport infrastructure even if this means mass unemployment in other regions of the nation.

When a private company tries to elevate its vested interests above the public interest, we tend to see through it. Most obviously, journalists are taught to treat the pronouncements of corporations and private companies with a degree of scepticism. However, as we have seen, charities enjoy a position of trust that most groups in society can only envy. This results in their being afforded a privileged "trusted expert" status in public and political discourse. The mere fact of being a charity is often all that is required to obtain prime media coverage irrespective of the nature of a charity's message or the robustness of the research behind it.

Few people within the media stop to ask is just how representative these charities are, and just who they speak on behalf of. It is doubtful that pressurised programme editors take the time to look at charities' annual accounts and reports to see how many ordinary members they have on their books, or how many small individual donors they enjoy the support of. If they did, they might be shocked at what they find. It turns out that many household name charities enjoy considerably less genuine public support than their privileged position in the media would suggest. And in many cases, they turn out to be dependent upon – and therefore beholden to – a single large funder.

While some rich philanthropists may be happy to donate large sums of money to worthy causes without seeking to influence the work they do or the public messages they transmit, they are in the minority. Influence is precisely what large donors seek – and get – in exchange for their financial support. Sometimes this is a direct "do as I/we want or you lose your funding". More often it is a matter of self-censorship by the staff and managers of charities – "we don't want to upset our funders".

The high degree of trust enjoyed by charities has left them vulnerable to the corrupting influence of funding from corporate donors who would struggle to get a sympathetic hearing if they sought to state their interests directly.

Astroturf charities

Charities' biggest weakness is that they depend on donations to survive. While we might like to imagine that charities make most of their money from thousands of public spirited individuals each making regular private donations, the truth is that most big-name charities depend on a handful of grants and donations from a range of wealthy individuals and organisations (including various departments of state).

In and of itself, there is nothing wrong with charities soliciting donations from wealthy donors. However, there is no such thing as a free lunch, and many donors want something in return. This might be no more than the warm feeling that almost all of us enjoy when we do something altruistic. More cynically, it may be a lawful means of avoiding tax or of using one's wealth to influence public debate.

It is very rare for a donor to make explicit demands on a charity. The bigger danger is the extent to which charities pre-emptively shift their goals and temper their message so as not to upset or alienate their big donors. When charities do this, they risk the charge that they have become little more than a publicly acceptable front for an otherwise less-reputable donor.

Health is the area where this problem has been most pronounced. So much so that debates around public health policy continue to be skewed toward the interests of a handful of large, corporate donors. For example, while cancer continues to attract the lion's share of charity donations and public funds, heart disease (a much bigger killer) has been squeezed out. The reason for this is simply that there are few profits to be made from drugs and treatments for heart disease, whereas a fortune can be made from any cancer drug that promises to extend life even by just a few months.

The pharmaceutical industry has a long track record of funding charities and patient groups in those areas where they produce and sell licensed drugs. Where such groups do not exist, the pharmaceutical industry has paid to set them up – hence the label "astroturf group" or "astroturf charity". Just like the artificial (astroturf) surface on many modern sports pitches, it looks real from a distance – it is only when you get close up that you discover that it is artificial.

Consider the Association of British Pharmaceutical Industry campaign strategy for persuading the UK and EU governments to relax the ban on direct-to-consumer advertising of prescription drugs[23]:

> "Now the ABPI has announced that it is launching the final stages of a campaign before it tackles the Government and the EU head on ... It is the spearhead of a carefully thought-out campaign. The ABPI battle plan is to *employ ground troops in the form of patient support groups*, sympathetic medical opinion and healthcare professionals - known as 'stakeholders' - which will lead the debate on the informed patient issue. This will have the effect of weakening political, ideological and professional defences ... Then the ABPI will follow through with high-level precision strikes on specific regulatory enclaves in both Whitehall and Brussels." (My emphasis)

Most often, pharmaceutical companies donate significant sums to existing charities. However, they are not adverse to setting up patient groups of their own:

[23] Jeffries M., The Mark of Zorro, Pharmaceutical Marketing, May 2000, 4-5.

"A pharmaceutical company will tomorrow break new ground by encouraging the public to demand that the NHS pay to make available one of its drugs. The campaign, Action for Access, is funded by Biogen and organised by a PR company on its behalf. It will urge multiple sclerosis sufferers to demand their health authorities agree to prescribe beta-interferon on the NHS, a very expensive drug, which can help some sufferers, but not all.[24]"

"The National Alliance for the Mentally Ill (NAMI) – 'a grassroots organisation of individuals with brain disorders and their family members' - received $11.72 million from 18 Pharma companies, between 1996 and mid-1999. NAMI's leading donor was Eli Lilly, maker of Prozac. They gave £2.87 million during that period"[25].

"The drug companies have also spent millions over the past decade to create seemingly independent groups that promote their agenda. Last year, the industry trade group created Citizens for Better Medicare, which has been waging a $50 million advertising campaign against a government-controlled prescription drug benefit. And lobbying records show that the drug companies are major

[24] Boseley S, *Drug firm asks public to insist NHS buys its product*, The Guardian, 29 September 1999.

[25] Silverstein K, www.motherjones.com/mother_jones /ND99.NAMI.html Prozac.org, MOJOwire magazine, Nov-Dec 1999.

backers of the Alliance for Better Medicare, which describes itself as 'a coalition of nearly 30 organizations representing seniors, patients, medical researchers and innovators, doctors, hospitals, small businesses and others'[26]."

In 2005, a Parliamentary Committee report[27] into the activities of the pharmaceutical industry noted that: "pharmaceutical companies use patient organisations as 'conduits to promote their products in a subtle form of marketing'. This leads to a situation in which, instead of representing the interests of patients, groups 'become marketing tools for the pharmaceutical companies'. Referral by the pharmaceutical industry to patient organisations as 'ground troops' for lobbying Government to increase access to new drugs is further evidence of this". The Committee recommended that:

"Patient groups should declare all significant funding and gifts in kind and the Government should seek to make appropriate changes to charity law to ensure this. It would in any case be greatly preferable if patient groups were funded by companies' charitable arms, rather than by companies themselves".

At the time of writing, this recommendation has not been

---

[26] Gerth G, Stolberg SG: *Drug industry has ties to groups with many different voices*, New York Times, 5 Oct 2000.

[27] House of Commons Health Committee. *The Influence of the Pharmaceutical Industry*. Fourth Report of Session 2004–05.

acted on, and charities continue to accept donations and gifts-in-kind from pharmaceutical (and other) corporations without having to declare the potential conflict to their donors or beneficiaries.

Astroturf charities – whether partially or fully funded by private interests – are a problem in all areas of public debate, as they give the impression of representing a genuine constituency rather than the direct interest of the industry, corporation or private individual behind them. For example, the GMB trade union recently complained about a range of groups that use charitable status and tax reliefs to promote the policies of the Conservative Party:

> "GMB, the union for public service workers, today called for the law to be changed to stop front organizations using tax relief gained by having charitable status to axe grind in favour of Tory Party policy.

> "The organizations with charitable status misusing tax reliefs are Reform, Social Affairs Unit, The Institute of Economic Affairs and The Countryside Alliance Foundation, The Politics and Economics Research Trust (Taxpayers Alliance) and ARK.

> "What most people won't know is that these so-called independent think tanks, which are able to claim charitable status, are actually funded by the companies who benefit from privatisation. They get money from companies like Capita, BUPA, KPMG,

Serco, Sodexo, PA Consulting to bankroll Reform and similar front organisations to keep peddling anti- public sector messages"[28].

Corporate-funded groups purporting to be about personal freedom have sought to influence such diverse policy debates as those around tobacco, Sunday trading, climate change and GM food. The objection to this is not that such campaigns are mounted, but that they misuse what any reasonable person would take to be "charity" as a means of sugar coating what would otherwise be seen for what it is –privileged vested interests arguing for their own ends.

Sock Puppet charities

Using charities as a front for delivering messages that might otherwise be viewed with suspicion by the public has proved so successful that politicians have climbed on the bandwagon. Indeed, public trust in politicians is so low that this strategy has almost become the modus operandi for policy debate in modern Britain.

More than 27,000 UK charities – many of them household names – depend upon public funding for more than three-quarters of their annual income. This raises serious concerns about their ability to properly represent the needs and views of their beneficiaries. There are even those who argue that such charities are little more than a trusted mouthpiece for expressing the views of discredited politicians.

[28] GMB Press Release - *GMB: stop fake charities like Reform funded by tax reliefs axe grinding for Tory party policies.* Monday 10th September 2012

The state-funded equivalent of an "astroturf charity" is known as a "sock puppet charity". There are many more of these, and they are as damaging in their own way to the public interest as those that act as a front for private interests.

For the most part, the state has provided funding in the form of unrestricted grants to those charities that promote safe and/or desired policies. On occasion, just like the pharmaceutical industry, the state has established its own sock puppets.

In the post war years, the state (with the best intentions) set up a series of "Councils *for...*" to work *on behalf of* people with a range of impairments or disabilities. These were not Councils *of* the various groups that they claimed to speak for. Nor did they rely on the support of such people (through membership or donations) to stay in business. The Councils *for...* continue to exist and continue to receive significant funds from the state. They also attract considerable criticism from genuine grass-roots groups of disabled people who argue that the very act of claiming to speak for disabled people perpetuates discrimination by sending out the message that disabled people cannot speak for themselves.

In practice, disabled people cannot get their voices heard in political debate because sock puppet charities drown them out. The Welsh Government provides an extreme example of how this process works.

Perhaps because of its underdeveloped economy, and successive Labour-led governments' failure to invest significantly in economic development, Wales has not attracted the kind of big business lobbying that has become such a problem at Westminster. However, because of the generous unrestricted grants given to favoured charities – especially those operating in health, education and social care – Wales has a serious, but unacknowledged problem with lobbying by state-funded sock puppet charities. To give just one example: The Welsh Assembly Cross-Party Group on Disability provides an opportunity for Assembly Members (AMs) with an interest in disability to meet with disability groups to get a better understanding of the situation and needs of disabled people in Wales. AMs in the group pass on the concerns raised to their parties and their AM colleagues. Ultimately, the concerns raised can result in changes to legislation, funding and service delivery throughout Wales. The groups represented on the Group at the time of writing were:

o   Learning Disability Wales
o   Mind Cymru
o   Disability Wales
o   Wales Council for Deaf People
o   Wales Council for the Blind

It is worth considering the extent to which these groups depend upon – and are thus beholden to – the Welsh Government[29] (based on the latest versions of these organisations' annual accounts):

Organisatn	Total Income	Direct Welsh Govt. Income	Indirect Welsh Govt. Income	Percentage of income from the Welsh Govt.
Learning Disability Wales	£764,701	£353,400	£68,000	55
Disability Wales	£545,559	£442,000	£15,800	84
Wales Council for Deaf People	£204,819	£134,535	£800	66
Wales Council for the Blind	£232,711	£145,350	£7,280	66

Each charity represented on this policy group receives more than half of its annual income from the Welsh Government. Much of the remaining income comes in the form of grants from the Big Lottery and from a range of grant making trusts. Individual donations are a small proportion of these organisations' total income, suggesting that they do not enjoy anywhere near the degree of public support that their regular meetings with political leaders would suggest.

---

[29] Mind Cymru is not a legal entity, but is the charity equivalent of a trading name used by the National Association for Mental Health. Total government grants to that organisation amounted to £4,630,000 of which, £556,000 came from the Welsh Government, which is likely to amount to over half of the income of Mind Cymru.

I don't doubt that each of these organisations can point to the good work that they do, and to the high degree of beneficiary-engagement they can carry out as a result of the funding they receive from the state. However, I do ask how content we would be if the only bodies participating in an important Cross-Party Group received between 55 and 85 percent of their annual income from, say, the pharmaceutical, petrochemical or tobacco industries?

For the most part, lobbying by state-funded organisations is in line with (some of) the needs of beneficiaries. The problem is that these charities will selectively choose to raise only those issues that are also in line with (or at least not opposed to) government policy. As such, this type of lobbying offers the shadow of democracy and public participation without its substance.

It is worth noting that many smaller disability groups – particularly those led by disabled people themselves – struggle to get an audience with politicians and decision makers. When they do, their views are seldom given the same weight as the views of the state-funded charities that enjoy the luxury of employing PR professionals and managers. For example, the Disabled People's Direct Action Network have expressed frustration about the role of charities:

> "These charities are not run by us and not controlled by us yet they claim to speak for us... Charities have become the major stumbling block to disabled people's freedom running many of the

institutions that segregate us from mainstream society.

"Whilst local and national disabled led organisations struggle to make ends meet national charities often pay executives £100,000 a year plus. Disability Rights campaigners are also concerned that when it comes to talking to government the charities are often willing to sell out disabled people. Disabled People and their organisations should be talking to government not the un-elected unaccountable charities who have a vested interest in denying our freedom"[30].

Nor is this problem limited to disability charities. In a pamphlet for the left-leaning Bevan Foundation, Sarah Lloyd-Jones and Chris Johnes[31] argue that over-reliance on Welsh Government funding has had a chilling effect on the democratic process in Wales while simultaneously preventing the development of genuine grass-roots charities and groups that would enable people to speak up for their own interests.

With both private and state funding of charity comes the risk that charities tone down their campaigning in order to please their funder. But there are even greater dangers when the state uses public funds to create the shadow of a charity sector while undermining its substance.

---

[30] www.johnnypops.demon.co.uk/poetry/articles/dan/pr-oct-2003

[31] *The Future of the Voluntary Sector.* Bevan Foundation 2014

Libertarian commentator Christopher Snowdon argues:

"Government funding of politically active charities, NGOs and pressure groups is objectionable on three counts. Firstly, it subverts democracy and debases the concept of charity. Secondly, it is an unnecessary and wasteful use of taxpayers' money. Thirdly, by funding like-minded organisations and ignoring others, genuine civil society is cold shouldered in the political process"[32].

It would be easy to dismiss Snowdon's arguments as libertarian extremism were it not for the fact that, following the election of a right-wing coalition government, many on the left are now raising the same concerns about state funded charities that promote otherwise unpalatable right-wing political views. Moreover, many of those who reject these concerns in relation to state-funded charities are often the first to raise exactly the same complaints when charities are dependent upon big business for their funding. For example, in 2011, environmentalist George Monbiot wrote a critique of state-funded charities that campaigned on a range of controversial right wing issues such as curbs on abortion, promoting selective private education, and denying climate change science[33].

The groups investigated by Monbiot are something of a

[32] *Sock Puppets: How the government lobbies itself and why.* IEA Discussion Paper No. 39. June 2012

[33] www.monbiot.com/2011/09/12/think-of-a-tank/

double whammy; heavily funded by corporate interests, but also registered as charities and enjoying state funding and support, these groups are quite correctly viewed as a threat to democracy.

So both left and right have, by different routes, arrived at an understanding that the way in which charities engage in political campaigning is a threat to democracy. All too often, vested interests in corporations and/or within an increasingly unaccountable political class use "charity" as a front for promoting views and causes that would otherwise be rejected out of hand by the public.

At present, it is hard work to find out if a charity has genuine widespread support from a large number of private individuals or if it is entirely dependent upon the largesse of one or two vested interests. Hence there is a clear need for the Charity Commission to change the rules on charity accounting both to force charities to declare any significant private donations and the total number of individual donors in any year.

The demand by MPs for commercially-funded charities to publicly state the proportion of their income that comes from this source is echoed in demands for a new system of regulation for state-funded charities. Nick Seddon[34] suggests creating three new categories of charity:

1. Independent Charity – receiving less than 30% of its

[34] *Who Cares? How State Funding and Political Activism Change Charity.* Civitas: Institute for the Study of Civil Society London. February 2007.

income from the state

2. State-Funded Charity – receiving 30-70% of its funding from the state

3. Statutory Agency – receiving more than 70% of its funding from the state.

It doesn't take too much of a leap of imagination to see that this system could be amended to suit both left and right within the debate by including commercial donations alongside state funding:

1. Independent Charity – receiving less than 30% of its income from the state or commercial organisations

2. Corporate-Funded Charity – receiving 30-70% of its funding from large commercial interests

3. State-Funded Charity – receiving 30-70% of its funding from the state

4. Statutory Agency – receiving more than 70% of its funding from the state

5. Corporate Agency – receiving more than 70% of its funding from large commercial interests.

Such a system would allow the public, beneficiaries, donors and broadcasters to decide how far the views of a particular charity should be treated as independent within public discourse.

However, it might be simpler to convert those charities that depend upon state funding into arms-length public bodies with directors appointed by Ministers (and thereby subject to the rules governing behaviour in a public office) and who, as a result of their public appointment, would be accountable to Parliament[35]. A change in charity accounting rules could then be used to make explicit how much income a charity receives from corporate interests.

Those organisations currently receiving state funding that wished to remain charities rather than convert to QUANGOs would be free to do so simply by handing back their public funds or finding replacement funding elsewhere.

More controversially (although most democratically), we could resolve the issue at a single stroke simply by tightening the definition of charity to exclude campaigning altogether. This would not (and should not) prevent groups from campaigning and speaking freely on any issue of concern. They could still lobby politicians, promote their cause in mass media, hold conferences, events and demonstrations, and carry out all of the other political practices that we associate with a democratic society. They just would not be able to refer to their activities as "charity", and would not be afforded the privileges of charitable status.

This seems to be the direction of travel for the Charity Commission. Rather than backing a change in the law, the Charity Commission has issued amended guidance on campaigning[36] which makes it much harder for charities

---

[35] This would also solve the issue of payments for trustees who oversee the biggest (usually state-funded) charities, since many public appointments are remunerated.

to engage in campaigning activities unless these are included in the charities "objects" as set out in their application to register as a charity. To be a charitable activity, campaigning would need to pass a "public benefit" test. Because successive governments have failed to define "public benefit" this has become a developing area of common law. Recently the Charity Commission has revised its position on the public benefit of political campaigning:

"The courts have taken the view that they are not in a position to judge whether or not a 'political purpose' is for the public benefit (and therefore whether or not it is charitable) because:

o the courts have no means of judging whether a proposed change in the law, or the policies of a political party, or a policy or decision of government, local authorities or other public bodies, will or will not be for the public benefit

o it is for Parliament, not the courts, to decide matters of public policy and changes in the law "[37].

Taken at face value, this revised guidance means that all but the most general campaigning by charities would fail the public benefit test, since nobody can know in advance whether the status quo or the proposed change is in the

---

[36] *What Makes a charity?* CC4.

[37] See Appendix B of the revised CC4 at: www.charitycommission .gov.uk / detailed-guidance/ registering-a-charity/ what-makes-a-charity-cc4/ annex-b-about-political-purposes/

public interest. This means that any charity campaigning that involves the promotion of either change or the status quo cannot be a charitable activity.

Charities are also coming to terms with the coalition government's Lobbying Act 2014, which seems likely to prevent a great deal of campaigning activity in the 12 months before a general election. That government felt bold enough to make this change, and that charities have not been able to effectively mobilise support against it is a measure of chrities' lack of genuine public support. As we have seen, most of the biggest charities gave up mobilising large numbers of donors many years ago in favour of attracting generous state and corporate donations. And rather than seeking to bring about the change they wish to see from the grass roots, too many charities have sought to use the state against the public. The result is that the public has proved largely indifferent when the government decided to curb the activities of charities.

While curbs on charity campaigning may have a chilling effect in the short-term, they do hold the potential to weed out the vested interests. The campaigns that are most likely to suffer are those where charities act as a front for vested interests (whether state, corporate, or just those of charities' paid employees). These campaigns involve a large amount of spending precisely because the charities involved do not enjoy an active supporter base that can be mobilised behind their campaigns. Genuine grassroots campaigns are built by the people for the people. They will not fall foul of the caps on campaign spending because grassroots movements do not require any single body to spend large sums of money; just consider the manner in which a campaign message can go "viral" on social media.

Moral Entrepreneurs

The sociologist Howard S. Becker first coined the term "moral entrepreneur" to describe people who seek either to make social rules or to enforce them:

> "The prototype of the rule creator... is the crusading reformer. He is interested in the content of rules. The existing rules do not satisfy him because there is some evil that profoundly disturbs him. He feels that nothing can be right in the world until rules are made to correct it. He operates with an absolute ethic; what he sees is truly and totally evil with no qualification. Any means is justified to do away with it. The crusader is fervent and righteous, often self-righteous"[38].

Such individuals are drawn to campaigning, and often gravitate toward charities that provide a platform from which to run campaigns – where such charities do not exist, moral entrepreneurs will happily set them up. In a lecture to the Adam Smith Institute, Christopher Snowden analysed the modus operandi of moral entrepreneurs in prohibition movements since the 19th century. He argues that all moral entrepreneurs stay more or less faithful to a five part campaigning strategy:

1. Create the evidence for the campaign – the term

[38] Howard S. Becker, 1963. *Outsiders: Studies in the Sociology of Deviance.*

"create" is used deliberately because campaigners will at best cherry pick those parts of the evidence base that support their case while ignoring anything that contradicts it, and at worse will simply invent evidence.

2. Attack the industry (e.g., alcohol, gambling, and tobacco) rather than individuals in order to de-personalise the campaign. This allows the subsequent debate to be framed in terms of "people v profit" or "David v Goliath".

3. Create a moral panic – use a single extreme example or handful of rare cases and encourage people (often through media manipulation) to believe that they are common and present a real threat.

4. Bring children into the campaign in order to rebut any liberal concerns about individual freedom and the dangers of allowing the state to interfere with individual liberties. While it is hard to persuade governments to regulate or ban alcohol, cigarettes or junk food, it will be much easier if you can persuade them that children are being harmed in the process.

5. Also to ease concerns about personal freedom, introduce the idea (using the created evidence) that failure to act harms everyone. For example, that allowing people to eat junk food is the cause of a raft of health problems that are straining the NHS.

At the time of writing, a charity called the National Obesity Forum has been in the news making claims about a future obesity epidemic that, they say, will only be prevented if the state steps in and introduces sugar and fat taxes, and bans anything that exposes children to the dangers of junk food. Whatever the rights and wrongs of the wider argument, this case is interesting precisely because it follows the five-point plan to the letter. The "evidence" turned out to be invented – when challenged by a BBC Radio 4 *More or Less* reporter, the author of the report admitted that he had made up the evidence! The attack was on a profiteering food industry rather than millions of people who actually enjoy the occasional burger, fizzy drink or doughnut. Moral panic tactics were used to try to claim that the next generation will be plagued by obesity. The campaign focused on the potential harm to children. And, of course, the campaign argued that the drain on health services would have a huge impact on the NHS.

Unfortunately, the mainstream media (which all too often lacks scientific rigour) presented the story pretty much at face value. It took the BBC Radio 4 *More or Less* statisticians to demonstrate that the "evidence" was based on a single outlier (an unexpected result that bucks an overall trend) in a single survey a decade ago, that suggested that obesity rates would be much higher than they actually are. In fact, the overall trend is toward far fewer cases of obesity in future than was claimed (although obesity remains a major public health issue). More or Less also took the time to examine the National Obesity Forum accounts posted on the Charity Commission website – in addition to finding that the charity was lax in meeting the legal requirement to post accounts on time (usually a sign of a seriously mismanaged organisation), they discovered that the charity was heavily reliant on donations from the slimming and diet industry. In short, the activities of the National Obesity Forum are indirectly as much about encouraging us to pay for (or get the NHS to pay for) various corporate slimming programmes, aids and potions as they are to do with preventing obesity by promoting healthy eating and exercise.

The common flaw with many moral entrepreneurs is that they lack the skills necessary to take campaigning to fruition and beyond. They lack political skills, making them easy prey to the kinds of vested interests that will take advantage of the good reputation of a charity for their own ends. For example, pharmaceutical companies that form alliances with campaigning health charities, or government officials who use the state to back-up campaigns for otherwise unpopular changes to legislation. Moral entrepreneurs particularly lack the legal skills required to draft good law. So, either they succeed in creating bad law (such as the Dangerous Dogs Act) or, again, they become the willing dupes of other vested interests (such as the Las Vegas gambling industry's support for anti-gambling legislation in neighbouring California).

As with charities that wilfully act as a front for vested commercial or state interests, those operated by moral entrepreneurs are anti-democratic. Indeed, moral entrepreneurs tend to be even more disregarding of the public interest. For example, anti-abortion and animal rights campaigners have even resorted to acts of violence and terrorism to pursue their particular interests. Less extreme groups disregard civil liberties developed over hundreds of years in their (often state-funded) drives for ever more draconian powers to interfere in the public's day to day lives.

In the last analysis, moral entrepreneurs treat the public with contempt. Rather than conceding that people can hold legitimate alternative views, the moral entrepreneur sees those people who disagree as plain stupid – at best someone to be educated, and at worst someone to be legislated and regulated into submission.

Perhaps the biggest threat to society posed by moral entrepreneurs stems from their inability to step outside their own moral framework. Most are what psychologists call "authoritarian personalities" – they are people who internalise and behave according to laws and rules irrespective of whether or not these rules are fair and just. They fail to understand that the majority of us have different personalities. Many among us are hedonistic personalities, and don't really care what the rules say. They are going to do those things that bring immediate gratification without worrying about possible future consequences. Others are gamblers – they will take calculated risks with rule breaking where they believe the benefits will outweigh any potential sanctions (think of the thousands of motorists who break the speed limit every day). Others are more liberal personalities, seeking to lawfully challenge and undermine laws and rules that they believe are unjust or that limit individual freedoms.

Moral entrepreneurs with authoritarian personalities are a major danger because they support and empower organised crime. They do so directly and unconsciously. For example, while nobody within the US temperance movement in the late 19th and early 20th century would have consciously supported the creation of organised crime networks, prohibition – the ultimate aim of the temperance movement – created mafia gangs and gangsters like Al Capone. Without a mass market for the illegal supply of alcohol, organised criminals would not have been able to raise the funds to develop their networks. Prohibition was also responsible for creating serious harm to people's health. Prior to prohibition, most US drinkers used beers and lagers. But these contain relatively small amounts of alcohol and are bulky, and thus hard to conceal or transport. Spirit, by contrast, can be highly concentrated in order to make it less bulky and in order to massively increase the per volume price. So the many US citizens who chose to ignore the law and seek out alcohol had to turn from relatively innocuous beer and lager to the highly risky spirits provided by the bootleggers. Moreover, once alcohol was illegal, all societal controls to regulate its quality were also removed. And since the aim of the criminal gangs who manufactured and distributed alcohol was to make money rather than to satisfy the end user, it became common to mix cheaper industrial alcohol in with the spirit they were selling in order to lower the cost of the ingredients.
Prohibition was a major factor in creating corruption

within law enforcement agencies. Perhaps inevitably, publicly funded police officers tend not to be highly paid. They are certainly not paid enough to put their lives on the line to intervene in what otherwise would be a consensual transaction between the buyers and sellers of alcohol. Indeed, the more farsighted law enforcement officers were only too aware that the only result of their impounding illegal alcohol and arresting bootleggers was to drive up the street price of alcohol and to clear the way for a rival gang to move in. For a minority of law enforcement officers (from all ranks) it was easier to accept a bribe to look the other way.

Today we see exactly the same problems in the so-called "war on drugs". Refined drugs like heroin and crack cocaine are easier to distribute and their concentration means they provide the best per-volume return on investment. Their illegality prevents regulation, so many of the users who are killed die as a result, in effect, of a lack of quality control – from an inability to see what dose they are taking, or from toxic additives being mixed with the drug to increase the return on the dealer's investment. The war on drugs has created international drug cartels that have become so sophisticated that much of their funds are laundered through legitimate businesses in the US, UK and EU.

Thus far, the UK authorities have stopped short of banning tobacco and alcohol. Nevertheless, there are warning signs of what prohibition would bring and, indeed, what may occur if government oversteps the limits of taxation[39]. For several decades people in the UK have been travelling to mainland Europe to buy alcohol and cigarettes without having to pay the UK duties. However, with mainland European prices now equalising with those in the UK, a more alarming trend has developed. We have witnessed a massive increase in bootleg spirits (some containing industrial alcohols that can kill and maim drinkers) being made and sold to undercut the regulated alcohol market. We have also seen gangs turning from using hydroponic "farms" to grow cannabis to using them to grow tobacco which can be sold at a much lower price than the regulated tobacco that has been taxed.

The activities of moral entrepreneurs often have other, less obvious negative consequences. Consider the public health industry. Over the years, the charities and corporations that benefit from allegedly promoting public health have successfully convinced politicians and civil servants that the reason for poor public health is a lack of information and education. This perspective undoubtedly plays into the prejudices of a governing class that is increasingly detached from the wider public. It also seems to be backed by statistics that show that the poorer you are, the less healthy you are likely to be. But it is a false perspective – and many of the people within government, health professions, charities and corporations know that it

---

[39] Although taxing unhealthy products can help to prevent people from taking them up, and encourage users to give up, this can only occur where taxes do not dive prices high enough to create space for a viable black market.

is false. The single biggest predictor of health/disease is not simply income, but the degree of inequality in society. Indeed, the British and USA upper classes (who live at the apex of grossly unequal societies) have significantly lower life expectancies than the upper classes in more equal nations such as the Germany and Sweden. More worryingly, many of those who benefit from promoting this dominant public health perspective are all too well aware that health information and education do not work. As public health expert Professor Sir Michael Marmot recently pointed out:

> "We know it is close to useless to lecture people about living healthily. Just telling people, 'eat well, don't get fat and drink in moderation' is useless – it's a waste of breath. It's correct, but it's a waste of breath"[40].

Nevertheless, public health bodies, egged on by moral entrepreneurs in health charities continue to justify their salaries by persuading politicians that the reason public health education doesn't work is that we haven't done enough of it. As Einstein famously noted, "insanity is doing the same thing over and over and expecting things to turn out differently".

Nor is the public health industry the only area where the campaigns of moral entrepreneurs have created an expensive and largely ineffective bureaucracy. From child protection to the environment and from education to

[40] Radio 4 *Today* programme, 4th February 2014.

antisocial behaviour, the state has created and grown a series of unaffordable bureaucracies that constitute an undemocratic and largely unaccountable infrastructure of welfare.

The charity moral entrepreneur cares little for either truth or the public interest – she sees her chosen cause as far too important to allow such apparently trivial matters to get in the way. She will gladly conflate vast numbers of people with less than optimal wellbeing with the much smaller number of people with severe mental illness in order to claim that one in four people have mental health problems. She sees no reason for her new cancer drug to go through the rigours of an approval process (designed to regulate safety, effectiveness and cost), and is unconcerned when it turns out that the drug results in the premature death of one in ten users, and costs the same as the annual running cost of a comprehensive school for each patient who receives it. She will urge government to overturn civil liberties on the grounds that it is better for ten innocent men to face jail than for a single guilty man to be acquitted.

Moral entrepreneurs' fetish for legislation is, in effect, an attempted shortcut designed to avoid hard work. Rather than harness the available resources (something that less developed societies than ours do despite their disadvantages) and mobilise public support in order to bring about change on the ground, they believe that problems can be solved overnight simply by passing a law. However, many recent changes in legislation barely touch bad behaviour (not least because law enforcement agencies don't have the resources to enforce existing laws, let alone new ones) but they do serve to bring the law into disrepute, they create more criminality as increasing numbers of people flout laws, and ultimately they empower an increasingly authoritarian state to usurp ever more power from the people.

Once one begins to dig below the surface (for example by examining a charity's accounts and annual reports) one often finds that moral entrepreneurs have a very small supporter base, relying more on state and/or corporate largesse than genuine support from ordinary members of the public. This is at the heart of why so many charities have become undemocratic – they step in where there is no public support, and call on (and thereby empower) the state to act against (or at best in the absence of) the public interest.

No matter what the cause, the damage done to democracy by empowering the state against the people is always a greater harm.

Charities as Businesses

All a charity used to have to do to raise money was to draw attention to the plight of its beneficiaries. Put up a poster of a disabled child, a starving African or (especially) an abandoned animal next to a collecting tin, and people would give money.

There then followed the series of funding scandals that continue to blight many charities. In the worst cases, fundraisers were passing on less than 10 percent of the money they raised to charity, with the rest going on "administration". The Charity Commission was forced to oblige charities to show their administration and fundraising costs separately in their annual accounts. And many donors today regard more than 15 percent of total spending on administration to be excessive[41].

Paradoxically, at the same time as they were being told to keep their administration costs down, charities were coming under greater pressure to be more "business-like"; often a euphemism for "professionally administered".

In fact, organisations' administration costs will (and quite rightly should) vary according to the activities they engage in. And "admin" should not be equated with

---

[41] It is likely that the public hostility to "admin costs" is actually a proxy for hostility to someone being paid for an activity that most believe should be voluntary. This is of course particularly scandalous when a "fundraiser" is paid more than 90% of the charity funds that he or she generates.

"waste". As Caroline Fiennes points out[42]:

> "'Admin' includes systems for capturing learning, for improving, for reducing costs. It's spending on those things which enable good performance. Scrimping on them is often a false economy."

The use of the term "business like" was unfortunate. It was lazy shorthand for being well run, responsive and effective. As Deborah Allcock-Taylor notes[43]:

> "We may have robust financial management systems, sophisticated strategic planning, audited annual accounts, paid employees and detailed organisational policies. We may even generate our own income through trading. But we're not businesses."

This is important because many charities have strayed into the business world.

For example:

> "Oxfam is the biggest second-hand book retailer in Europe. It has launched a book festival. It has released a series of books with top-name authors. It is behaving like a very good income-earning charity.[44]"

---

[42] http://giving-evidence.com/2013/05/02/admin-data/

[43] www.dsc.org.uk /PolicyandResearch /news / charitiesarenotbusinesses

Celina Ribeiro suggests a double standard in which we want charities to be businesses so long as they stay poor. However, the real double standard comes from organisations that want to enjoy all of the tax-free benefits of being a charity while simultaneously undercutting legitimate private businesses that have at least as valuable a social purpose as do the charities. When a charity is exempt from corporation tax and reaps 100% relief on business rates, an independent business simply cannot compete. Operations close, jobs are lost, older and less able customers are left without access to shops, and everyone loses out.

In practice, the main reason why most small shops have failed is the competition from big supermarkets, out of town retailers and a growing online retail sector rather than competition from charity shops. And rather than withdrawing reliefs from charity shops, it would be easier to address the problem by providing business rates relief to small businesses, social enterprises and other local bodies where these benefit the local economy. Indeed, it would be more sensible to target rate relief at any small organisation (irrespective of its legal status) that operates within a local economy, while also charging higher business rates to any large organisation (including the big charities) that sucks resources out of the local economy.

This said, there is another important regulatory failure

[44] Celina Ribeiro, *Charities should be business like, but not successful.* Civil Society 2009.

here. In law, charities are only meant to enjoy tax relief on their trading activities if these are either small (no more than £50,000 for a big charity, and as little as £5,000 for a small one) or directly related to the delivery of their charitable aims. Since for example, selling second hand books, clothing and furniture is unlikely to be a charitable aim in its own right, HMRC should be doing much more to tax the income that charities derive from these activities.

HMRC and the Charity Commission have been encouraging charities to establish subsidiary trading companies to operate shops and other business activities. Tax can then be avoided if the trading company donates its profits to the charity. However, this does mean that the charity would lose the business rates relief on any trading premises. There have also been some concerns with the trading arms of charities where directors are paid (sometimes a substantial proportion of the trading income) but where the trading arm and the charity are indistinguishable to the public.

Arguments about business rates relief on charity shops have been raging for many years. But the same concerns are now arising where charities are venturing into new public service contracts. A key driver for this was the dramatic shift in the late 1990s in the way the state funds charities. For most of the post-war period, governments have supported charities by providing direct aid in the form of unrestricted grants in those areas (e.g., health, education, economic development) that they wished to promote. This was only lawful because charities were not businesses and so grants could not be regarded as a state subsidy.

However, in recent years the state has moved away from grant funding. Instead, charities have been encouraged to tender to deliver a raft of government services, especially in the employment and criminal justice sectors. These public sector contracts can be highly lucrative. For example, one national charity has an annual income of £28.5 million - £25.5 million of which comes from fulfilling public sector contracts for which it competes with a range of ordinary businesses (not a single penny of the charity's income comes from public donations). Another national charity raises £41 million out of a total income of £53 million from delivering public services (just £700,000 comes from fundraising and donations). This raises important questions about whether a business activity that generates several million pounds should enjoy corporation tax exemption and business rates reliefs that other organisations that tender for the same work do not enjoy. These tax reliefs probably amount to a breach of EU State Aid legislation, since they amount to a generous state subsidy for one type of organisation that is not received by its competitors. Since State Aid penalties can be applied retrospectively and are notoriously harsh, this amounts to a serious risk to any charity that engages in public service delivery.

Tax reliefs should also not be taken for granted. The question of tax relief is determined not (as far too many people assume) by the legal status of the organisation, but whether the public service is also a "charitable activity" in law. To be so, the activity must:

o   Fall within one of the 12 "heads of charity" set out in the Charities Act 2011, and
o   Be for public benefit, and
o   Be a stated object of the charity delivering the service.

Although the origins of many public services are in charity, one cannot simply assume that a public service is also charitable. Many public services do not fit within the 12 heads of charity. Simply having them *delivered by* a charity does not change this.

And even if a public service can be fitted within one of the 12 criteria, one cannot assume that it will be for public benefit. The problem here is that nobody has satisfactorily defined what is meant by "public benefit". As the Attorney General makes clear[45]:

> "The authorities do not provide a comprehensive statement of the public benefit requirement but provide rather a series of examples of when the public benefit requirement is or is not satisfied. There is no application of some overarching, coherent, principle by which the Courts have been guided".

---

[45] Attorney General v Charity Commission (The Poverty Reference) [2012] WTLR. 977 at [34].

Without clarity about public benefit one cannot differentiate between a food bank, the local corner shop or a large supermarket chain – each could argue that it distributes food *for the public benefit*. It is only their legal structures that distinguish them, and it is clear that simply being carried out by a charity does not automatically mean that an activity is charitable.

A crucial test is whether a service or activity excludes "the poor"[46]. If a service is free at the point of delivery, this should not be a problem. However, if a charity derives its income from charging for public services that it operates, it must ensure that the charges do not prevent people of modest means from accessing it. Indeed, a large supermarket chain (least likely to be viewed as "charitable" by the public) could argue that by using its control of the supply chain to drive down prices and by providing a non-profit "value range" of loss-leading essential foods, it is of greater "public benefit" than many charities.

The objects of a charity are the biggest legal barrier to its operating a public service as a charitable activity[47]. Few charities were established to operate as businesses that tender for public service contracts. As such, they must often seriously bend the terms for which they were

[46] A rule initially introduced to challenge the charitable status of some private schools, although it is worth noting that the used clothing and furniture sold in some charity shops in more affluent areas is now so expensive that the poor can no longer afford it.

[47] It is unlawful for a charity to carry out activities that fall outside its objects even if the activities are charitable and of public benefit.

established in order to operate in this way. And this poses a serious potential risk. While the government is currently urging charities to tender for public service contracts, HMRC may not be so kind in future.

In tax law, a charity can only qualify for corporation tax exemption on its trading activities (such as delivering a public service) if this is directly related to its charitable objects. For example, an education charity would not have to pay tax on money it makes from tuition fees, but it would be liable for tax if it made significant income from, for example, letting its rooms to tourists during vacations. If the political climate does change, HMRC may begin to ask whether the delivery of public service contracts is sufficiently close to charities objectives to exempt them from corporation tax.

In the present climate, charities enjoy a significant competitive advantage over their competitors when it comes to tendering to deliver public services. However, a more profound question is whether charities should be delivering public services at all. While charities should try to be "professional" in working effectively to meet their aims, they are not businesses:

> "We need businesses to be profitable. We need them to make money so that they can employ people, pay corporation tax and contribute to the wider fiscal economy. However, that is not the purpose of charity. For business, money is the end, the ultimate measure of success. For charities,

money is only ever the means and for around 150,000 charities (those with turnovers under £100k pa), it's not even that much of a means. For us, money is a tool to help us serve our beneficiaries or deliver against our cause, and that is all. And when we forget that – when we lose sight of what we are trying to do in the struggle to survive or when we believe that success is about the size of our turnover or the amount of reserves we have accumulated, then we have not just lost the point – we've lost the plot"[48].

There is considerable concern that too many charities are setting their charitable purposes aside as a result of the inherent conflicts of interest that arise from the employment of staff and the need to manage excess funds. Because while the law imposes severe restrictions on how charities manage funds and how they relate to paid employees, there is little de-facto regulation to force them to stick to their charitable ends. Furthermore, "he who pays the piper calls the tune". And where the state is paying, it restricts charities that should be speaking out on behalf of their beneficiaries. As Zoe Williams reports:

"A charity sector reliant on government contracts would find it difficult to criticise government policy... Sometimes, it's because there are gagging orders in government contracts. It's not a matter of discretion; it's a matter of law. Other times, they self-censor, on the basis that this dance never ends

[48] Debra Allcock Tyler - *Charities are not businesses.*

– they will always be bidding for new contracts. The need to be looked on favourably by the UK Border Agency, or the local authority, or the Department for Work and Pensions, will never go away"[49].

The role of and importance of charities in civil society has been their ability to find innovative solutions to social needs that are not being addressed – or at least not effectively so – by the state or the market. But the more charities are brought under the umbrella of public service provision, the more conservative they are obliged to be. Rather than encouraging the state and the market to do things differently, charities sign contracts obliging them to do things as they are.

As early as 2007, a report for the Charity Commission found that:

> "Charities that deliver public services were significantly less likely to agree that:
> - o their charitable activities were driven by their mission rather than by funding opportunities;
> - o that they were free to make decisions without pressure to conform to funders; or
> - o that they involved their trustees in decisions about what projects or activities to undertake"[50].

[49] *Charities' silence on government policy is tantamount to collusion.* Guardian, 22 January 2013.

Dependence on the state, either directly or through a sub-contract to a government supplier like Capita, G4S or Serco means that charities have no option but to put the needs of their beneficiaries far below the terms of the contract:

"In the past decade, national and local government grants to charities and the voluntary sector fell by a third to £3bn. Over the same period, the amount received in the form of service delivery contracts went up from £4.5bn to £11.2bn. A small number of the largest charities are, wittingly or not, actively complicit in the ideological dismantling of the NHS and statutory social care services, for their own gain, while simultaneously sacrificing their independence and ability to advocate on behalf of the vulnerable"[51].

In the care sector, for example, charities have been forced to use zero-hours contracts and to undercut the minimum wage in order to deliver the unrealistic care services demanded by cash-starved local authorities. Consider this statement from a leading national social care charity:

"Due to a shift in the way health services are commissioned, like many charities, we have started

---

[50] Charity Commission (2007) *Stand and Deliver: the future for charities delivering public services.*

[51] Ally Fogg, *The charity sector has problems, but executive pay is hardly the worst.* Guardian, 19 September 2013

using zero-hours contracts for a very small number of our services in some areas...

"The new 'personalisation' of social care means that some people with mental illness are now given personal budgets to buy their own care direct from providers, including charities like us.

"This means we no longer receive block funding from local authorities for a set period of time, making it impossible for us to guarantee work for our staff through traditional contracts. Without the use of zero-hours contracts, we wouldn't be able to carry on providing support to people who need it".

The problem is that as local authority budgets have been squeezed, so cost cuts have been passed onto the companies and charities that deliver public services to end users. This has meant that charities are increasingly unable to meet the needs of their users without cutting wages and relying increasingly on the unpaid labour of their volunteers. In the face of cuts, some charities and their supporters have begun to question whether charities should be engaged in the social care system at all. In Liverpool, for example two charities – Local Solutions and Person Shaped Support – have chosen to pull out of the system, arguing that:

"As a charity we need to work for the higher good for our staff and beneficiaries. We have got empathy with the public sector, and it has huge financial problems, but someone needs to say that enough is enough...[52]"

Similar issues have been raised in relation to government Workfare initiatives that require long-term unemployed and disabled people to work for their benefits. Peter Beresford has highlighted two key problems with charities engaged in these programmes:

"First, many charities have lost sight of their traditional value-base, and become indistinguishable from the state and private sectors. They have become permeated by their personnel, ways of working and ethics. But they lack the accountability of public services and the preoccupation with the bottom line of for-profit provision. This can leave them with little of their own that is positive. Second, an independent advocacy role – charities' unique selling point – tends not to sit comfortably with securing public service contracts, especially when the state is the main commissioner. But as grants have dried up, it is largely through providing services that charities seek to achieve financial security. Workfare is a major case in point"[53].

In practice, it is only the minority of super-charities that

[52] Annette Rawstrone, *Two Liverpool charities reject local authority contracts over reduced levels of service.* Third Sector, 26 November 2013

[53] *Why did large charities embrace the government's work schemes?* Guardian Professional, 12 March 2012

can take full advantage of government contracts and/or operate successful trading businesses. But these trading activities are creating similar inequalities in the so-called "third sector" as those found in the private sector. At the end of 2013, just 1.2 percent of charities in England and Wales held 69 percent of the sector's £65bn annual income, while 75.2 percent of charities (those with incomes below £100,000) shared just 3.5 percent of the annual income. It is no accident that much of the demand for charity trustees to be paid – something that would totally undermine the voluntary principle that makes charity unique – comes from the tiny minority of charities with annual incomes above £5 million. Indeed, the compromise position put forward by the Association of Chief Executives of Voluntary Organisations (ACEVO) was that *only* the trustees of these super-charities should be paid.

In reality, the ACEVO position is more an admission that is impossible for a charity to engage in big business without ceasing to be charitable. The need to manage huge budgets, large numbers of paid staff, and an army of volunteers means, inevitably, that the super-charities have to employ senior managers on six figure salaries that compare to similar roles in the public and private sector. Even then, these charities continue to experience problems at a strategic level because they cannot attract suitable trustees without offering the kind of salaries required by people who sit on the boards of directors of similar sized private companies.

Rather than undermine the voluntarism at the very heart

of charity by allowing a handful of trustees to be paid (and presumably starting an arms race in which trustees compete to obtain remuneration similar to that paid to the directors of City of London firms) we would be better served by simply converting the largest state-funded and public-service-delivering charities into private limited companies or genuine QUANGOs whose appointed (paid) directors would be bound by the rules governing conduct in a public office, and who would be properly accountable to Parliament.

In recognising the gulf that has opened up between the largest charities and the rest, we see that for the few, being "business-like" has served to create self-interested national (and sometimes international) uber-charities that put the needs of their (often highly-paid) core staff and the wishes of their government paymasters far ahead of the needs and wishes of the beneficiaries they claim to serve. In the process, they have shed much of the morality that had separated charity from both the state and the private sector. They have also tarnished the "charity brand" to the disadvantage of the overwhelming majority of charities that do not employ paid staff, and are more firmly embedded within the communities that they serve. Most alarmingly, their discredited example is being widely touted as a model for smaller charities to follow.

The Self-Defeating Cycle

In December 2013, the BBC broadcast a *Panorama* documentary outlining the contradiction between the aims of Comic Relief and their investment of charitable funds in the arms and tobacco industry. This was the first time that mainstream media had made an examination of the investment practices of the big charities (those with sufficient reserves to invest). However, the apparent contradictions in Comic Relief's approach to investment lie at the heart of the way a great deal of charitable activity in the UK is funded.

All but the smallest of charities rely to some extent on grants from grant-making charitable trusts. These trusts were usually established either as a corporate responsibility arm of a major corporation, or in the will of a wealthy philanthropist with the aim of supporting charities that serve particular beneficiary groups. However, these trusts were not established simply to distribute all of their money. Rather, they were created to invest the money so that the interest earned could be distributed as grants to qualifying charities. This sounds reasonable enough until you begin to ask about where, exactly, charitable funds have been invested. As the world discovered to our cost in 2008, the modern global financial system has become so complex that nobody can be altogether sure where their money is invested. And as Comic Relief discovered, there is no guarantee that investments will be ethical.

Indeed, even investment in so-called 'ethical funds' does not necessarily guarantee that funds will be invested ethically. As Simon Read notes:

> "Ethical funds attract investors by refusing to invest in so-called "sin" stocks such as pornography, alcohol and gambling. But research by Fair Pensions shows that many ignore equally contentious issues such as child labour, fossil fuel and support for oppressive regimes"[54].

Moreover, there is no obligation for 'ethical funds' to disclose the companies that they invest in. Nor do they generally take an active role in improving the behaviour and practices of the companies whose stock they hold. In practice, ethical investment usually means avoiding the very worst companies (as defined by the fund management) rather than only investing in the very best.

Charities do have some leeway when it comes to making investments. Unlike companies that have a duty to *maximise* the return on their shareholders' investment, charities are only required to *optimise* the return on their investments. This is a subtle distinction, but it does allow charities to decline to invest in some areas of the economy if this would be likely to harm their reputation (and thus result in a drop in future donations). For example, health charities can refuse to invest in tobacco, alcohol and junk food, while landmine charities can refuse to invest in arms

[54] *Is ethical investment really that ethical?* Independent, 8 December 2012.

companies that manufacture these weapons.

Unfortunately, there is no requirement for charities to make public details of their investments. As a result, while the public can see how much income a charity derives from investments, there is no way of knowing where a charity has invested its donors' money. For example, we do not know for sure whether Comic Relief continues to invest in tobacco, the arms trade or any other suspect industry, simply because the charity changed the way it reports its investment income so that it is impossible to tell.

Insofar as this issue has become part of public discourse, it has been about whether or not it is ethical for a charity to invest in a particular company or industry. There might be a case in favour – for example, investment in the arms industry might bring in enough income to fund the removal of all landmines, while investment in tobacco might provide the resources needed to create a cure for cancer. Somehow, this seems unlikely, but it is an argument that could be made.

But what if the problem is more systemic? In recent years, public anger has been directed against several global corporations such as Starbucks and Amazon that are seen to be ducking their responsibility to pay (corporation) tax in the countries where they operate. In doing so, they benefit from the public funded infrastructure, education system and public health and welfare, without directly contributing. And in less well developed areas of the world, global corporations are a lot more ruthless in extracting resources while putting little (if anything) back into the systems that they plunder.

This raises a deeper question about the investment of charitable funds – what if the problems charities have been created to address are directly caused by the global corporations and nation states (through investment in government bonds) where charities invest their donors' funds? What if the global capitalist (i.e., corporatist) system – of which charity investment is a part – is responsible for the social problems for which charity is needed?

If this is the case, then we need to carry out a serious cost-benefit analysis. Because investing in corporations or states that cause social problems may well do far more harm to the beneficiaries of our charity than can be mitigated by distributing the proceeds of that investment in the form of grants.

Of course, in the real world, the situation is made worse by a raft of intermediaries who must be paid their share of the return on investment before any beneficiary gets to see any resources:

o   Investment managers
o   The charity's staff
o   Aid sub-committees
o   Project managers
o   Local staff and suppliers

All are an additional part of the infrastructure of welfare, and each takes their cut out of the return on investment before any end user benefits from the charity's investment. This opens up a similar question to the one I posed about state pensions and benefits payments and the growth of a bureaucratic "infrastructure of welfare" – might we be better off scrapping the whole infrastructure and simply giving the money directly to the end user?

In the case of charity investment, might we do less damage by withdrawing charity and charity donors' funds from the global corporate financial system and instead invest directly in helping beneficiaries to sustainably help themselves?

Is it time for a different model?

In many ways, the third sector is a mirror of much that is wrong with our wider society. There is huge inequality between the vast majority who must eke out a living on less than 5 percent of total charity income, and an increasingly bloated minority that holds nearly three-quarters of the funds. And just like the corporate and political elite, the elite super-charities are as contemptuous of the public that they claim to serve. Indeed, along with the bankers, tax dodging corporations and expenses-fiddling MPs, the charity elite no longer see a need to garner public support for their causes. Instead, like the elite in general, they see the best way of sustaining themselves lying in adding to the public debts that already have to be paid by heavily overburdened future taxpayers. Why live within your means when there is a public purse to be raided?

There is much to be criticised in the charity sector. But it would be a cop-out simply to blame the petty self-interest that drives fraudsters, moral entrepreneurs and ordinary employees. Nor should we simply point an accusing finger at the Charity Commission's failure to adequately police and regulate charities. We should not allow our concerns with charities to descend into an argument about public spending on regulation either. These are all major issues. But they mask a bigger issue – public passivity. For too long, we have used charity as a way of assuaging our consciences. We put our spare cash in a rattling tin, donate used goods to charity shops and do silly things for various telethons. Having done so, we sit back with a warm contented feeling and congratulate ourselves for being charitable. But if you are donating to a charity whose trustees or staff are fraudsters, then *you* are part of the problem. If you have given money to a charitable campaign that treats the public with contempt by empowering an authoritarian state against the people, then *you* are part of the problem. If you contribute to the causes of moral entrepreneurs who lie, invent statistics and trample on the broader public interest, then *you* are part of the problem.

We are all part of the problem when we limit our engagement with our communities and the charities that claim to serve them. From the multi-million pound tax dodging of The Cup Trust to the Director of Plas Madoc Communities First defrauding the charity (and indirectly the people of Wales) right down to the lowliest charity employee who purloins a pocket full of biros and post-it notes, public passivity is at the heart of what is wrong with charity.

None of us should donate to a charity without first looking through its accounts and annual returns. These are easy enough to obtain at no cost from the Charity Commission website. Poorly managed charities are now red-lined on the website, indicating that donors would be better served supporting other charities. Charities are also required to make declarations about who funds them and about the charitable activities they engage in. They must also declare whether and how much they pay employees, and whether trustees are paid. While individual donors may find this onerous, it is essential that corporate, state and charitable foundations go out of their way to understand the charities that they fund. Indeed, there is a social need for donor-funded audit and investigation organisations that can carry out unannounced inspections and audits of a randomly selected proportion of charities as a means of ensuring that donors' money is being used appropriately. This could be done by establishing an audit and investigation division, part-funded by donors, within the Charity Commission. Alternatively, major donors (including the state) could contract private audit and investigation organisations to check that their funds are being spent appropriately.

We should also vote against those political parties that continue to fund charities directly from the public purse, or look the other way when charities fail to pay their fair share of corporation tax on their income from delivering public services. After all, there is little likelihood of these charities turning down public funding of their own volition.

Mass media could do much more too. Journalists are generally sloppy in their coverage of charity. There is a tendency to view charities as White Knights on the side of all that is right and good, valiantly protecting an undefended public against attack from the abuses of state and corporate power. But all too often, it turns out that the loudest charities are the voice of the state and/or corporate power, and that the public needs to be protected from these charities. Again, at the very least, journalists should take 15 minutes to look through a charity's annual accounts to see whose interests the charity represents. And where – as with the National Obesity Forum – it turns out that the charity appears to be dependent on corporate funding, journalists should ask them to defend this. In the same way, journalists need to be much more critical of state-funded charities. They might ask why, for example, the state heavily funds charities made up of able bodied people who claim to speak for disabled people, but seldom supports charities led by disabled people themselves. Does this not exacerbate the stigma and discrimination that disabled people experience from those who assume that they are incapable of speaking for themselves?

Charities must take responsibility for changing the way they operate too. The "business-like" model that charities were encouraged to follow has failed. While it has made a small elite group of uber-charities wealthy and often indistinguishable from private government contractors like Capita, G4S and Serco, it has left the overwhelming majority of charities struggling to make ends meet and increasingly unable to deliver their services. Continuing to follow this model will result in more of the same. As cuts in public services bite, and the public sector asks charities to shoulder more of the pain, so more charities will go to the wall. Meanwhile, as tendering for contracts to deliver public services becomes the main means of survival, then only the very biggest charities will be able to prosper.

But as the snouts of the super-charities dig ever deeper into the state and corporate funding troughs, so they become ever more distant from the public whose trust they rely on. Increasingly, these charities treat individual donors with contempt, preferring to mug them in the street or through unsolicited telephone calls or cold calling. Increasingly they see volunteers as unpaid employees to be used and abused rather than as their most valued resource. Like any other organisation whose income is not derived from their consumers, the super-charities are more concerned with pleasing their state and corporate paymasters than with meeting the needs of their beneficiaries.

Rather than emulating this approach to charity, the majority of charities should play to their biggest strength – their ongoing connection with the communities they serve. Small charities should shun the quick fixes of state funding and legislation-driven behaviour change in favour of the harder (but ultimately much more powerful) practice of building genuine communities of interest from the grass roots.

The fact is that there are two enormous untapped resources in our society – our beneficiaries (the people that charities exist to serve) and our wider communities. And it is the smallest charities and community groups that have the greatest potential to harness these resources. To the super-charities, active beneficiaries are to be feared. If beneficiaries are able to speak and act for themselves – *and they are* – then we don't need bloated organisations to speak and act *for them*. And where communities become active participants in charitable and socially meaningful activity, they too discover that much of the infrastructure of welfare that includes the state, the super-charities and the corporations that profit from the delivery of public services will prove to be unnecessary too.

Community and beneficiary engagement is not easy and there are few quick wins – this is precisely why so many charities have chosen to campaign for changes in the law, and to accept state funding instead. But it is increasingly clear that the current model is failing and, despite claims to the contrary, this is a systemic failure rather than "a few bad apples".

If we want to build the ideal of charity – of communities voluntarily and altruistically looking after our own – then we need to work together to change the model. And if this makes the people who run and work for charities uncomfortable; good! The role of anyone who runs or works for a charity must be to make themselves redundant by solving the problem for which they were established.

Innovation is often the essential ingredient that charities can bring to bear on social problems. However this innovation is most often the preserve of small, connected groups, and contrasts with the conservatism of risk-averse super-charities whose existence depends upon maintaining the status quo.

There will of course be critics who will argue that some problems simply cannot be solved at a small or local level. And they are right. More than a century ago people had realised that the social ills that followed industrialisation and the shift from a rural to an urban population would never be solved through a combination of parish relief and charity. Education, pensions, health and housing required (and require) public provision that harnesses the resources of the whole nation. However, the intrusion of charities into these areas has helped fuel the remorseless withdrawal of public provision of, and government responsibility for, these essential services.

I do not doubt that we need everything from social housing to medical research. Rather, it is my contention that these things should not be the preserve of charities. If (and it is a big *IF*) private businesses can run public services more effectively than direct public provision, I have no problem with this happening... so long as the government is always held accountable. Indeed, I believe that there is a case to be made for developing and employing not for profit social businesses (co-ops, CICs, etc) to deliver public services. However, this is not the place for charity.

The future of charity is in an alternative and genuinely voluntary model based on mobilising beneficiaries and the wider community to bring about the improvements that many charities were established to achieve but have all too often lost sight of. This will involve hard work. But we have seen to our cost what happens when charities seek to short-cut the process.

Also by Tim Watkins:

Smart Fundraising: A Guide to Fundraising for Small Charities and Community Groups

No More Panic!: A Guide to overcoming panic attacks and recovering from panic disorder

Helping Hands: How to Help Someone Else Cope with Mental Health Problems

Depression Workbook: 70 Self-help techniques for recovering from depression

Food for Mood: A guide to healthy eating for mental health

The Hidden Epidemic: An examination of suicide in the UK

Residential homes: Quality of life and quality of service

In Deep Water: an investigation into problems in the aftermath of the North Wales ("Towyn") floods of 1990

www.ingramcontent.com/pod-product-compliance
Lightning Source LLC
Chambersburg PA
CBHW070155290526
45789CB00002B/776